AAI Awards 2004

NEW IRISH ARCHITECTURE 19
AAI AWARDS 2004

Published to coincide with the AAI Awards
2004 touring exhibition, at the Guinness
Storehouse, Dublin, April 2004.

Edited by John O'Regan and Nicola Dearey

© Architectural Association of Ireland and
Gandon Editions, 2004. All rights reserved.

ISBN 0948037 075

Produced by Gandon Editions for the AAI.

design	John O'Regan
	(© Gandon, 2004)
production	Nicola Dearey
	Gunther Berkus
photography	see page 198
printing	Betaprint, Dublin
distribution	Gandon Distribution
	and its overseas agents
	(for back-issues, see p 144)

GANDON EDITIONS
Oysterhaven, Kinsale, Co Cork
T +353 (0)21-4770830 / F +353 (0)21-4770755
E gandon@eircom.net
visit our web-site: www.gandon-editions.com

front cover – A Way to School – Ardscoil Mhuire,
Ballinasloe (*illustrated*) and NKEC, Celbridge
(Grafton Architects)

The AAI and Gandon Editions are not
responsible for the views expressed herein.

The AAI and Gandon Editions
are grant-aided by

The Arts Council /
An Chomhairle Ealaíon

ARCHITECTURAL ASSOCIATION
OF IRELAND

The AAI was founded in 1896 "to promote and
afford facilities for the study of architecture
and the allied sciences and arts and to provide
a medium of friendly communication between
members and others interested in the progress
of architecture."

MEMBERSHIP

Membership of the AAI is open to architects,
architectural students, and anyone interested
in architecture. Annual membership rates are:
– full member: €60
– student / unwaged / associate org.: €15
Applications for membership should be sent to
the Membership Sec. at the address below.

COMMITTEE 2003-2004

President	Gary Mongey
Vice-Pres / Hon Sec	Miriam Dunn
Hon. Treasurer	Shane McEnroe
Committee	Susie Carson
	Paul Clerkin
	James Corbett
	Michael de Siún
	Donal Hickey
	Peter Kable
	Maxim Laroussi
	Aoibheann Ní Mhearáin
	Anna Ryan
	Rachel Scanell
	David Smith
	Noelle Sweeney
	Derek Treneman
Student Reps	Michael Bannon, DIT
	Deirdre Brophy, UCD
Administrator	Caroline O'Hanrahan

ARCHITECTURAL ASSOCIATION OF IRELAND
8 Merrion Square, Dublin 2
T +353 (0)1-6614100 / F +353 (0)1-6614150
E aaiadmin@eircom.net
visit our web-site: www.archeire.com/aai/

NEW IRISH ARCHITECTURE 19

AAI AWARDS 2004

DUBLIN FROM A BIRD'S-EYE VIEW

AARON BETSKY

Caught between collage and concrete fetishism, is there hope for Irish architecture? That is the question thrown up by the results of the 2004 AAI Awards programme. The answer, of course, is yes, but it would seem only if it manages to escape from its current rather insular condition. The range of 'good' work, as represented by the submissions the jury saw, does not seem to move much beyond the twin legacies of James Stirling on the one hand, and Louis Kahn on the other. A few Miesian moves here, a Mirallian curve there, and the picture we, as a jury, were presented is complete. Is that really all there is? Why is this the case? Does this work have a clear relation to its physical, economic or social context? These are questions an outside examiner, jetting in for a few days and confined to Dublin, cannot fully answer. What rests are a set of speculations.

Temple Bar – a quick descent from new cultural district to boozy neo-Soho

I had never been to Ireland, though I had long loved its literature, its art and its music. I was expecting a tourist presentation of snug and cozy streets, a kind of English provincial town made more pleasant by the local mores and traditions. The myth, it turns out, was just that. I caution to add that this does not mean that I was not impressed by the vivaciousness, energy and intelligence of the culture into which we dipped our toes for three days. What this does mean is that what we saw in the physical landscape of the country's largest city gave us pause.

What astonished me as a first-time observer was the poverty and emptiness of Dublin's physical environment. Of course Ireland is now a rich and prosperous nation, the food is good and the prospects of its well-educated citizenry better. But the stage on which this Irish miracle takes place is one that remains barren and ill-defined. The rows of ship's ballast brick façades looking out over Georgian squares and avenues that are too wide for their walls, the lack of focal points in the urban fabric, the uncontrolled miasma of traffic, and the quick descent of Temple Bar from new cultural district to boozy neo-Soho gave at least this visitor a sense of forlornness that no decoration or references to James Joyce could take away. The splendours of Dublin exist in an ephemeral sphere, in its literary legacy and its musical present, and inside the pub. Outside, there is not even a sense of faded glory, like, for instance, that of Lisbon or Budapest, to give one hope for a revival of the physical context.

There are, we are told, very good and sad historic reasons for this empty and mean condition. Ireland became depopulated, deforested, and raped of its natural resources through centuries of imperialist plunder. Its last period of native splendour was in the early Middle Ages, before the urban fabric could be set. One could even speculate that the current urban scenography, such as it is, is a response to the emptiness of the Irish landscape, translating its rolling hills and empty bogs into a city landscape in the same way that the towns of The Netherlands, where I live, densify that country's geometry of meadows, irrigation ditches, dams and dykes into a tight pattern of residential streets with few monuments or vistas.

One could also argue that the art of Ireland is a paean to this emptiness and sense of loss. A sense of imprisonment, the bitterness and the escape, either to another country or into an alcoholic realm where that same gloom has a golden sheen, speaks through in the paintings of Francis Bacon as well as the work of the country's great poets and novelists. But it does not speak through in its architecture.

The Spire – probably the best civic monument since Maya Lin's Veteran Memorial

The positive result of this situation is that there are also not that many egregious mistakes visible in the landscape. There are no great expressways cutting through the centre of town, nor is there a financial district that has usurped all life in favour of a fortress of glass and steel towers. Industry has not claimed vast stretches that must now be reclaimed. The rich do not live radically segregated from the poor, though there are distinct districts and slums. On the whole, the street patterns that have grown up since the Middle Ages, were enlarged in the 18th century, saw a 19th-century change in scale, and have since been expanded with terraces, housing developments and now suburban sprawl, are clearly legible as a collection of only slightly superimposed fabrics.

The vivaciousness of the public interior also gives this visitor hope. The pub (as a type) is better developed in Ireland than anywhere else. It appears to be a locus for social life, and its rambling, tightly packed forms have a quality that is markedly more intense – though difficult to describe in formal language – than its English, Germanic or French counterparts. The very poverty of the historic context makes the few rich rooms, or the few rich objects within those rooms, stand out even more.

There are, of course, also a few new monuments and hopeful signs. The Millennium Spire is probably the best civic monument to be constructed since Maya Lin's Veteran

Memorial of three decades ago in Washington. Its abstract, endlessly attenuated form gives lie to the often fussy complexity of most current architecture, and its shiny skin stands in strong contrast to the dreariness of the street out of which it rises to such majestic heights.

Yet these objects and spaces remain exceptions. Is the ground of Dublin too barren to produce great form? A superficial survey of the city – which, again, is all I offer here – would seem to confirm that thought. There are few great monuments that can match those of England or France, not in the Georgian style or in the modern mode. Even the touch-stone of Modernism, Scott's bus station, though a fantastic 'urban condenser', is tectoni-cally a confused amalgam of borrowed conceits patched together into a slightly uncomfortable collage standing rather forlornly at the edge of the more active part of town. Trinity College is a strange hybrid between an open campus on the Oxbridge model, and a hodge-podge of buildings squeezed together with no apparent rhyme or reason. The river has not been so much reclaimed by urban design as it has become less of a barrier.

Now that Ireland has enough money to build, it does not seem to have much of a tradition to fall back on. What grandeur there is present was and still feels imported, like the renovated seat of government. So Dublin architects, who seem to do most of the build-ing all over Ireland, have imported two modes in which they design. In themselves, these

Trinity College – a hybrid between Oxbridge and a hodge-podge of buildings with no rhyme or reason

styles or manners of approach express – and I apol-ogise for saying this – a provincial and tentative approach to the development of an idiom appropri-ate to this setting. They borrow bits and pieces of the past, create fragments of civic grandeur abstracted to meet modern demands, and never come together into a coherent and strong shape.

The first of these borrowed modes is the col-lage of historical forms and Modernist slices that marked the oeuvre of James Stirling. Several of the country's best practitioners worked or studied with Stirling, and his presence is more evident here than anywhere else in the world. Temple Bar is like a whole neighbourhood rebuilt according to his principles, namely as a collection of abstracted references to the existing context, mon-umental moments and openings that allow new activities to shelter under contemporary technology. The work of McCullough Mulvin Architects seems especially inspired by this way of working.

The second influence that appears to be dominant in Ireland today is the work of Louis Kahn. Here one of Kahn's collaborators was responsible for introducing his work to local architects. Grafton Architects, among many others, show that they have studied the concrete frames, wood infill panels and large geometric rhetoric of this Philadelphia mas-ter with great care. What is remarkable is that his Irish followers have lifted Kahn's manner of expressing himself whole, holding onto certain compositional techniques (the small window framed in pine wood panels, the expressed and attenuated concrete frames), even though the uses for these elements is radically different in the apartment buildings, schools and office complexes the Irish disciples design.

Together, these influences have shaped the dominant mode in which contemporary

Irish architecture operates. The result presents itself as a collection of fragmented geometries, a tectonic dominated by wood and concrete, an abstraction of historic forms, and a monumentalisation of standard building types through the use of geometry. At times, this Irish postmodernism shades off into more historic references, while at other times it fragments into an adaptation of what, ten years ago, was called deconstructivism. A more dominant counter-movement is that of a kind of minimalism, practiced by architects such as Hassett Ducatez and FKL, which seems to owe as much to the work of John Pawson as it does to Ludwig Mies van der Rohe.

The advantage of this consensus is that it has a clarity that allows it to be defined as Irish architecture. It also contains a restrictive palette, a catalogue of parts and 'moves' that one can imagine could be taught to a next generation of architects so that they can adopt and adapt it into a more coherent and native idiom. In a hopeful scenario, this vocabulary could transform itself into an authentic language of architecture, tied to history and material, that is capable of giving the forces defining building – which are, whether they are financial, regulatory or material, more and more global in nature – a local character. Here one would have to understand that local traditions are always dynamic, appearing as the result of importation and domestication rather than being bred into the bone.

What makes me wonder whether this can happen, and what I miss as an outside observer, is a sense of clear connection to what I observe in the physical landscape of Dublin and Ireland. Is there not some way that those rows of brick façades, without cornice or columns, those strangely one-sided streets, that undulating landscape of terraces, or even the deeper geography and geology of the Irish land could find a way to form? Is there not some way that the educational tools and the international applications to which that knowledge has been put could find its reflection in the built environ-

Georgian Dublin – rows of brick façades without cornice or columns

ment? Is an architecture equivalent of U2 possible? (Certainly it will not be the tower they have commissioned.)

For an outside reviewer, there is not much more to do than to ask such questions. Architecture takes time to develop, both because the building process is so slow and because it is part of everyday life, making innovation much more difficult to accept for its audience than it would be in the safe distance of a museum or in an evanescent world of sounds. Perhaps someday soon Ireland's new-found wealth will turn into a treasury of form that uses exactly the particular history and nature of the place to make a contribution to the way in which we understand our physical world and how we can shape it. This reviewer looks forward to that day.

The annual Tegral Critic's Lecture is sponsored by Tegral Building Products.

Assessors' Reports

AARON BETSKY, *architectural critic*

Contemporary Irish architecture seems to exist in a void. That, at least, is what is we must assume from the evidence we were presented with as assessors. Almost all submissions were careful to eliminate the context in which the buildings were placed, editing out the surrounding buildings, the sites and the slopes on which the physical artifacts no doubt stand. In addition, most architects also felt it important to give us as little information as possible about the functions, the entrances or the furnishings of the buildings they submitted. This makes our final judgment, at least in my mind, provisional.

In some cases, I would like to reverse our decision on seeing the physical object. In other cases I've no doubt that the actual building is considerably better than the evidence with which we were presented. New information I have received since about some buildings makes much of what I had doubts about in the presentation now seem eminently logical. In general, I would like to offer a strong plea both to the designers to provide the jury with more information, and to the organisers to find a way in which future jurors can see 'in the flesh' at least the group of buildings that appears most likely to win an award before making a final decision.

The awarding of the medal to Grafton Architects is as much a recognition of their continual and strong contribution to contemporary Irish architecture as it is confirmation that what they appear to have produced in these two schools is remarkable. The inventive use of space, the clear expression of structure, and the thoughtful way in which light, scale and material have been manipulated to create a humanly scaled educational community all deserve our highest praise. These schools, built on relatively tight budgets, show that Grafton's working methods can produce major contributions to the still-emerging architectural culture of this country.

Among the other awards, I would like to single out McCullough Mulvin's Tubbercurry Library and Civic Offices, if for no other reason than that the structure appears to be slightly odd. The discrepancy of scale between what seems to be a tiny community and the majesty of the complex's reading room, the amorphous space of the central circulation hall and the lack of hierarchy in forms, is carried through in an aesthetic that seems to continually deny any sense of certainty about what is important, how things are built, or where one should go. At the risk of over-interpretation, this would seem to me to be an apt way to approach and house civic structures in the early 21st century.

I am also encouraged by such small works as Alan Jones' Office for a Coffee Importer, whose economy of means achieves a great deal of effect. It is difficult to say how much of this is the result of clever presentation, but that is, in a sense, part of the point: by looking at the existing conditions in which he works and thinking about how it could be represented in a manner that mines the meagre surroundings for maximum effect, this young architect is showing an alternative way of creating architecture from the one evident in the work of most of the other submissions to the 2004 Awards programme.

I hope coming years will show an ever-increasing diversity in approaches to how the existing physical, economic and social conditions of Ireland can be translated into productive, reflexive and critical form.

AARON BETSKY was born in Missoula, Montana, in 1958, but moved to The Netherlands at an early age. He graduated from Yale University with a BA in 1979, and an M.Arch in 1983. He worked in the offices of Frank Gehry (1985-87) and Hodgetts & Fung Design (1987), and established his own practice in 1987. Between 1995 and 2001, he was Curator of Architecture, Design & Digital Projects at the San Francisco Museum of Modern Art, and became Director of The Netherlands Architecture Institute in 2001. He has taught and lectured extensively, and has published many books on architecture and design. He lives in Rotterdam.

EDDIE CONROY, *Irish assessor*

Economic growth has given rise to as many design awards as bad new buildings, but the AAI Awards remain a singular institution. The festival of teeth-grinding and garment-rending launched annually with the announcement of the AAI Awards may have declined, but the Awards remain a going concern. The commitment to a robust evaluation of Irish architecture against an international quality datum, embodied in the requirement for two visiting jurors, has ensured its continued relevance. This year the balance between Aaron Betsky and Paul Robbrecht, between reason and feeling, was powerful and instructive to watch. The judging process was careful, lengthy and frank. Consistent quality in format and content has established the Awards publication as a metronome of the stately tempo of Irish architecture, and it continues to be a valuable record.

Recent juries have carefully mapped the underlying consistencies of submitted projects. Foremost is an avoidance of demonstrative or overly expressive form, and a general tendency towards urban refinement and civic legibility. There is a concentration on the finer grain of urban conditions, and a liveliness in typological response. This sensitivity and care extends to schemes set in natural landscapes. There is also a developing commitment towards enhanced materiality (rooted in contemporary European work, but also in an ongoing interest in the work of Louis Kahn).

It is possible to view this consensus, this 'quiet emulation', as conservative. Even in a growing economy, buildings are still perceived as too expensive to act as experiments. Irish architects have not been drawn to the new ideas (physics, virtual-reality, topology, fractal mathematics) which inform work in other states. The pressures of mass procurement, industrialised construction, and large urban infrastructures have not impacted sufficiently as yet to demand a response. The critique of suburban disintegration enjoyed as value-free form-making or celebrated as retail hyperactivity has found few takers.

There is another view, however, that the work submitted is not conservative, but may be viewed as part of a radical and sustained ambition to forge an urbanism as a framework for envisioning and realising a liberal, inclusive and modern society. The early AAI Awards were held against a background of urban decay, zero growth and political stagnation. These projects were obliged to contain within themselves the seed of unbuilt urban morphologies into which the projects might one day sit. This commitment to meaningful urban intensity (a yearning for the European city – condenser of life, diversity) constitutes a form of politics, a response to the monocultural, inert nature of Ireland as it then existed. The seriousness of this intent is reflected in the seriousness of the work it generates. Incremental, careful and realisable, this work is an ongoing enterprise rooted in societal as much as artistic concerns.

In the current AAI Awards, the detailed urban-insertion projects no longer carry the seed of larger models. They now carefully calibrate the increment of space necessary for amenity and quality in tight urban sites, they celebrate and demand infill and densification in town and city centres.

The design of complex building types, such as the mixed-use public building in Tubbercurry, are confident in their role as urban regenerators, and point up the need to intensify rural town centres, avoiding the suburban sites normally reserved for them. (The design of good buildings on bad sites is one of the most depressing aspects of modern Irish design.) The clarity of response of the Ardscoil Mhuire project towards defining its position in the landscape is the antithesis of the ambivalence of weak urban edges now so common.

The shadows cast by these projects suggest the need for a more all-embracing normalisation of the urbanisation process. Urban form and urban life, now routinely doubted elsewhere, can still find meaningful reality here. This work is not the sole preserve of the architect, and requires the skills of other disciplines, but the level of serious care and respect embodied in the best of these projects continues to add quality and focus to this ongoing enterprise.

EDDIE CONROY FRIAI graduated from the School of Architecture, University College Dublin, in 1980. He has worked mainly in the public service, and is currently Senior Architect with South Dublin County Council, where he is responsible for special projects and urban design. He has been awarded the RIAI Silver Medal for Housing, and several regional design awards. He is particularly interested in social housing and the architecture of the early 20th-century in Ireland. He is a visiting critic at both UCD and DIT schools of architecture.

MARIAN FINUCANE, *distinguished non-architect*

It was interesting to participate on the adjudicating panel for the AAI Awards 2004. The more the public and the professionals are encouraged or harangued into insisting on higher standards in aesthetics in the built environment, the better.

In an era where an explosion of building occurred, and is continuing, there are still abysmal and depressing standards. However, there are also hopeful signs of improvement. One would hope that the more committed architects would be more forceful in articulating the necessity for better standards in all areas. In terms of these awards, having looked at some of the buildings in reality, post-adjudication, the presentation in terms of drawings and photographs did not always do justice to the buildings themselves.

Congratulations to all who organised and participated.

MARIAN FINUCANE was born in Dublin and educated at Scoil Chaitríona. She studied architecture at DIT Bolton Street, before joining RTÉ in 1974 as a television and radio announcer. She started working in programmes in 1976, and since then has worked in current affairs, religious affairs, women's issues, light entertainment, documentaries, books and media, receiving many broadcasting awards in that time. In 1999 she chaired a government committee on architectural awareness, and currently presents the Marian Finucane Show on RTÉ Radio 1.

ANTOINETTE O'NEILL, *Irish assessor*

I commend the Architectural Association as it continues into its twentieth year with this Awards scheme. The series of exhibitions and catalogues over the intervening years provide a narrative through a time of great growth and change in Irish architecture.

In 1985-86, the first year the Awards were run, the context for architecture in Ireland was informed by the still prevalent concern for the built heritage. There was a feeling that the grand and heroic gestures of contemporary architecture were being made elsewhere in Europe. In 2003 there is a very different canvas: the architecture made in Ireland has achieved confidence and maturity. Work by Irish architects has influence beyond this country, as evidenced by recent significant wins by Irish practices in international architectural design competitions; the successful presence of Ireland in the seventh and eighth architecture biennali in Venice; and by the inclusion of Irish design in many recent international periodicals. By introducing Irish architecture to international appraisal, the AAI has been a major catalyst in this internationalisation.

Irish work here has become comfortable with its place and relevant to its time. If the debate started in the mid-1980s was around the dual issue of Irishness and temporal relevance, then the architecture being made twenty years later has transcended these issues and reached a maturity out of them. The best examples of contemporary work we saw in this year's Awards were those which responded to the specificness of their brief and site, and generated something special out of these. In this respect it was very refreshing to see so many site conditions, including open rural sites, within the final 21 commended schemes.

Throughout the assessment, two issues gave rise to much discussion amongst the panel – the effectiveness of the presentation methods used, and the lack of site description or context definition in many cases. Both of these relate to the central issue of whether the assessors should visit a group of shortlisted schemes, an issue which I know is broached frequently by the AAI and assessors alike. The merits for such an approach are obvious, but when the process is presentation-based, it throws up interesting assessment criteria. It is significant, for instance, that the medal-winning entry for schools in Ballinasloe and Celbridge gave clear and relevant site information through text and drawing. This clarity belied the integral relevance of the site context to the work, and produced (most obviously in the case of Ballinasloe) a building of grace and light which accommodated its function with great elegance.

For me it was a privilege to be asked to assess the AAI Awards. I was moved by much of what I saw – the quality of light in the Mortuary Chapels at St James's Hospital; the powerful beauty of the Medical Research Laboratories at UCD; the controlled serenity of the Brick House in Dublin 6 – and provoking emotional response is what great architecture does so well.

I look to the future of the *New Irish Architecture* awards catalogues as they continue to tell the story of architecture in Ireland.

ANTOINETTE O'NEILL was born in Limerick in 1963. After graduating in architecture from University College Dublin in 1985, she worked in London for Rick Mather Architects and in Berlin for Architekturbüro ELW, before returning to Dublin to work for Derek Tynan Architects, and, later, the Office of Public Works (OPW). She has been a consultant on architecture to The Arts Council / An Chomhairle Ealaíon since 2000. In 2002 she contributed to the European Forum for Architectural Policies in Helsinki, and was instrumental in establishing one of Europe's largest awards for young architects – the biennial Kevin Kieran Award.

PAUL ROBBRECHT, *foreign assessor*

Dublin and Ireland have a special meaning for me because it was on a visit there in the late 1960s that I made the definitive decision to become an architect.

I was very much touched by the country, and I made a decision to return quickly and often. But it was 1992 before I got back, when the German artist Ulrich Ruckriem invited me. He lives in Bunclody, Co Wexford, where he preserves a part of his oeuvre in a magnificent shed-construction of steel and corrugated plate. This remarkable rural building, with its bent roof shapes, is a kind of typological coming together of rural architecture and industrial construction, such as was common in Ireland in the past.

During that visit I noticed here and there that new, quality architecture was being made by young architects, including many public buildings. However the work of the bigger Irish architectural practices remained unknown to me. In a short period I visited Ireland several times, and I took note of a particularly strong movement in Irish architecture. This movement is characterised by a uncompromised choice for enduring architecture, endurance that requires the hard landscape, a kind of stubbornness that sometimes turns itself into a well-thought-out elegance.

The more remarkable submissions for these AAI Awards were a series of public buildings – schools, university buildings and sports facilities. We could say that Ireland is interested in the young and the dynamic, but also that this stony country invests in enduring architecture – buildings that have to resist the stubborn conditions of the country. This was shown in the eulogised project of Grafton Architects – the schools in Ballinasloe and Celbridge – supporting constructions with a great openness to give the young place and space to develop and to meet.

The Cigar Box and the Brick House also grabbed my attention because they express the same decisive positioning. The almost informal project, Office for a Coffee Importer, also struck me because it made me think of unconsciously wandering through sheds and port areas (the beginning of an Irish short story?).

However, there should more attention paid by AAI Awards entrants to the presentation of the interior architecture of buildings. The interiorising is to me as important as the exterior. It tells what really is going on in the building.

It is very encouraging to see the effort Ireland is making by investing in new school buildings and universities, in which they are building a strong future.

PAUL ROBBRECHT was born in 1950. He established a practice with Hilde Daem in Ghent in 1975. Through their activities they search for the mutual relationship between art and architecture, and the office has collaborated with artists on many projects. Robbrecht & Daem Architects has won various prizes for their work, including the Flemish Culture Prize for Architecture (1996; together with Marie-José Van Hee), and the Culture Prize of the Catholic University of Leuven (2001). In 1998 a bilingual (Dutch/English) monograph entitled *Work in Architecture* was published by Ludion, and a new monograph on the practice is currently in production.

Registrar's Report

The Architectural Association of Ireland (AAI) was founded in 1896 'to promote and afford facilities for the study of architecture and the allied sciences and arts and to provide a medium of friendly communication between members and others interested in the progress of architecture'.

The AAI Awards were established in 1986 as 'an annual award scheme for excellence in architectural design'. The intentions of the Awards are:

– to encourage higher standards of architecture throughout the country
– to recognise projects which make a contribution to Irish architecture
– to inform the public of emerging directions in contemporary architecture

The Awards scheme is open to architects practising in Ireland and Irish architects practising in their own right abroad, submitting current projects and buildings.

Entries are judged by a panel of five assessors – an architectural critic, a foreign assessor, two invited Irish assessors, and a distinguished non-architect. For the AAI Awards 2004, the five assessors were: Aaron Betsky (The Netherlands), Eddie Conroy, Antoinette O'Neill, Paul Robbrecht (Belgium), and Marion Finucane (broadcaster).

In the AAI Awards 2004, the assessors awarded the Downes Bronze Medal, the Association's premier award for excellence in architectural design. They also made seven Awards and thirteen Special Mentions.

This is the nineteenth exhibition and publication in the series since 1986. The AAI Awards 2004 attracted 91 submissions. To date, the AAI Awards has attracted 1,230 submissions. The Medal has been awarded in 13 of these years – twice to projects and 12 times to completed buildings. There have been a further 101 Award-winners, and 199 Special Mentions. The annual AAI Awards exhibitions and books have featured a total of 308 buildings and projects by over 100 architectural practices.

The results of the AAI Awards are exhibited and published annually as *New Irish Architecture*. The series represents the most comprehensive documentation of the best of contemporary Irish architecture. Previous volumes in the series are available from good bookshops, or can be ordered from Gandon Editions (see page 199). For a history of the AAI Awards, and a listing of previous Award-winners and Special Mentions from 1986-1995, see *New Irish Architecture* 10 (AAI / Gandon Editions, 1995).

The AAI welcomes feedback to the exhibition and publication as part of the ongoing development of the AAI Awards as Ireland's premier annual architectural awards scheme.

— John O'Regan, AAI *Awards Registrar*

Invitation to Enter

ANNUAL AWARDS FOR EXCELLENCE IN ARCHITECTURAL DESIGN

INTENTIONS

— To encourage higher standards of architecture throughout the country
— To recognise projects which make a contribution to Irish architecture
— To inform the public of emerging directions in contemporary architecture.

ASSESSMENT

- A panel of five distinguished assessors is invited to make a broad selection of schemes which they feel would make a contribution to Irish architecture. The assessors comprise an architectural critic; a foreign architect; two Irish architects; and a distinguished non-architect.
- The Assessors' decision is final.
- The Registrar and the President of the AAI will attend the assessment as observers.

ELIGIBILITY

- The Awards scheme is open to architects practising in Ireland and Irish architects practising in their own right abroad.
- Current projects – including building, landscape and infrastructure works, competition-winning projects, and theoretical works – which are under development, under construction, or completed in that year are eligible.
- However, (i) student projects, (ii) projects carried out in the offices of the Assessors or the AAI President, or (iii) previous AAI Award-winning projects are not eligible.
- The Registrar's decision is final on the eligibility of submitted designs.

REGISTRATION

- Applicants who wish to submit more than one entry must return an additional entry fee for each entry.
- The architects credited with the design of any entry must be current members of the AAI.

SUBMISSION

- Entrants are invited to communicate their design to the public by drawings, photographs or other graphic representation, and to explain the project by the use of appropriate images and text
- Each entry is to comprise 1 or 2 panels mounted on rigid card (but not framed), either A1 or 594mm square.
- A descriptive text (1 page, 300 words max.) must accompany each entry. Entrants must declare in this text the size of the project (in m^2), and the stage the project is at (design / planning / under construction / when completed).
- Entries are to be anonymous, with the official entry form fixed in to the back of one of the panels. The supplied numbered labels should be fixed to the back of each panel, to the front of the descriptive text, and to the external packaging.

AWARDS

- The Downes Bronze Medal was donated to the AAI by Harry Allberry – a founder member – in 1905-06, to be 'awarded to the member who produces the best measured drawings and sketches of any building ... erected before 1820'. The award was discontinued in the early 1950s. The medal has been reintroduced as the Association's premier award for excellence in architectural design.
- There will be a maximum of 7 Awards. The Downes Medal may be awarded at the discretion of the assessors. Any eligible entry is eligible for the Medal. A number of entries may be selected for Special Mention.

EXHIBITION

- The Awards and Special Mentions will be featured in an exhibition travelling to venues around Ireland.
- Award-winners will be invited to submit additional material for exhibition. The exhibited drawings and models will be returned only after completion of the exhibition tour.
- There will be a catalogue published featuring Awards and and Special Mentions, with the assessors' considered written comments on each project. The AAI reserves the right to the editorial use of all material supplied by the architects of the Awards and Special Mentions.

The INVITATION TO ENTER for the AAI Awards 2005 will be published in September 2004. All current AAI members will automatically receive copies by post. Non-members can request copies from the AAI Administrator from that date (contact details on page 2).

Assessors

From 1986-1990, the 3-member jury comprised a foreign assessor and two Irish assessors (including the previous year's Medal-winner). From 1991-1999, the 5-member jury comprised a foreign assessor, three Irish assessors (including the previous year's Medal-winner), and a distinguished non-architect. Since 2000, the 5-member jury has comprised a foreign assessor, an architectural critic, two Irish assessors, and a distinguished non-architect. The architectural critic is sponsored by Tegral Building Products.

Wiel Arets			Felim Egan (artist)	1995	Rafael Moneo		
(Netherlands)	1996		Michelle Fagan	1996	(Spain)		1991
James Barrett	1995		Yvonne Farrell	1987	David Naessens		1991
Florian Beigel			Marian Finucane		Willem Jan Neutelings		
(Germany/UK)	2000		(broadcaster)	2004	(Netherlands)		1995
Ciarán Benson			Sheila Foley	2001	Esmonde O'Briain		1998
(psychologist)	1996		Kenneth Frampton		Joan O'Connor		1994
Aaron Betsky			(USA)	1997	Michael O'Doherty		2001
(Netherlands)	2004		Arthur Gibney	1986	Sheila O'Donnell	1989,	1998
Esteve Bonell			Michael Gold		Seán O'Laoire		1993
(Spain)	1990		(UK)	1988	Prof Cathal O'Neill		1996
Angela Brady	2003		Neil Hegarty	1988	Antoinette O'Neill		2004
Gerry Cahill	1996		John Hejduk		Fintan O'Toole		
Ross Cahill-O'Brien	1992		(USA)	1994	(journalist)		1993
Alberto Campo Baeza			Róisín Heneghan	2002	James Pike		2000
(Spain)	1998		James Horan	1992	Paul Robbrecht		
Gerard Carty	1992		David Hughes	1997	(Belgium)		2004
David Chipperfield			Michael Hussey	1997	Vivienne Roche		
(UK)	1989		John Hutchinson		(artist)		1994
Shay Cleary	1990		(gallery director)	2002	Jonathan Sergison		
Jean-Louis Cohen			Louisa Hutton		(UK)		2001
(France)	2001		(Germany)	2003	Dietmar Steiner		
Beatriz Colomina			Garry Hynes		(Austria)		2002
(Spain/USA)	2000		(theatre director)	2000	Sam Stephenson		1997
Eddie Conroy	2004		Jan Olav Jensen		Deyan Sudjic		
Peter Cook			(Norway)	2002	(Italy)		2003
(UK)	1993		Richard Kearney		Ronald Tallon		1991
Dorothy Cross			(philosopher)	1991	Peter Tansey		1999
(artist)	1997		Kevin Kieran	1998	Barrie Todd		2002
Edward Cullinan			Yves Lion		John Tuomey		1991
(UK)	1987		(France)	1999	Mark Turpin		2003
Michael Cullinan	1995		Tarla Mac Gabhann	2000	Derek Tynan		1987
Shane de Blacam	1994		Des McMahon	1989	Corban Walker (artist)		2003
Tom de Paor	1994		Edward McParland		Dorothy Walker		
Mary Donohoe	1993		(arch. historian)	1998	(art writer)		1992
Theo Dorgan (poet)	1999		Shelley McNamara	1999	Peter Wilson		
Noel Dowley	1993		John Meagher	1986	(UK)		1992
Mary Doyle	1999		John Miller (UK)	1986	Kevin Woods		1995
Peter Doyle	1990		Gerry Mitchell	1988			

AAI AWARDS 2004

A WAY TO SCHOOL

Ardscoil Mhuire, Ballinasloe, and North Kildare Educate Together Project, Celbridge

GRAFTON ARCHITECTS

North Kildare Educate Together Project, Celbridge; opposite – Ardscoil Mhuire, Ballinasloe

Two schools, one senior, one junior, in two different parts of Ireland, sit on limestone rock. Ardscoil Mhuire is a secondary school for 450 girls on the side of a gently sloping hill at the edge of the town of Ballinasloe in Co Galway. North Kildare Educate Together Project (NKETP) is a primary school for 250 children on a flat meadow, looking towards the Dublin Mountains, close to the village of Celbridge in Co Kildare. This ten-classroom school includes two specialised teaching classrooms for children with autism, and is the first custom-built integrated school in the country.

Designed and built simultaneously, 90 kilometres apart, these two schools explore the architectural possibilities of developing an approach to construction and to the use of the courtyard type which would be adaptable to two quite different contexts and two quite different scales and schedules of accommodation. The Department of Education & Science requires that schools are generally single-storey and are constructed in exposed concrete blockwork. This is a given constraint. Within these constraints, together within the rigid

cost limits, we discovered the potential of using a precast-concrete roof. The rationalisation for this construction method actually liberated the design, and produced buildings with a sense of weight, which was important to us.

A Matter of Degree

We worked within the maximum structurally allowable pitch of the precast-concrete roof slabs, which is between 4° and 7°. We laid this roof like a blanket on the plan. A 7.2m x 1.2m grid spans between classroom walls, and one or two planks are omitted to form 1.2m or 2.4m light-scoops and ventilation chimneys. In north Kildare, because the site is flat, a valley was formed when the minimum floor-to-ceiling height was reached. Ballinasloe pushes its floor plate into the hill, allowing the roofscape to run parallel with the slope and to form renewed contour lines. Here the roof, which is level with the ground at the back of the site, is thought about as a continuation of this ground. The 'fault line', which is formed by the retaining wall separating lower and upper-level classrooms, is reflected in the roof plan, and determines the location of the central light-scoops. NKETP, anchored to the flat ground, has a copper-clad wave-like roof, with the light chimneys reaching to the sky.

End Result

While the approach to construction had to be very precise and rational, the resultant volumes formed by this heavy roof, depressed or lifted to form lightboxes and ventilating chimneys, modify and animate the rigorous and economic plans. The environment created is full of light, with cross-ventilation for each classroom. The efficiency of the roof as a light and air filter meant that areas of glazing in walls could be reduced. Windows were then placed to frame ground views and sky views. Transparency, through and across each plan, connects the community of each building to each other.

Outside Inside Courtyards

Each plan is carved, hollowed out by courtyards – inside-out rooms with the sky as the roof. In NKETP, protected, intimate indoor and outdoor spaces are formed, where children connect with their own classroom and garden, and are involved in creating their own immediate world. The spaces are measured both internally and externally for use and ownership by the individual and by small groups. In Ballinasloe, designed for older students, the larger community of the total school is more singular, and within this community the student is more mobile and independent.

Ardscoil Mhuire, Ballinasloe, Co Galway
Area – 4,200m². Stage – completed January 2003.

North Kildare Educate Together Project, Celbridge, Co Kildare
Area – 1,800m². Stage – completed May 2003.

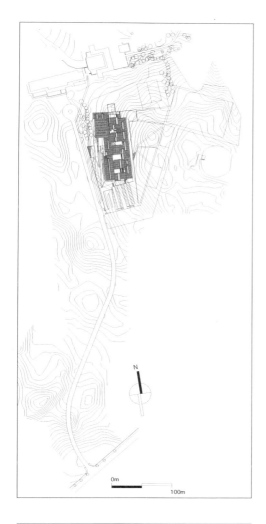

Om
100m

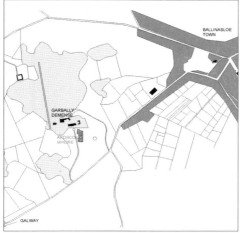

ARDSCOIL MHUIRE, BALLINASLOE

Topographically the site is made up of a thin layer of clay, following a sloping bed of limestone rock. Given the nature of this particular site, the building follows this sloping limestone bed, and therefore the actual experience of the hill is maintained by the new building, absorbing the memory of the original undulating landscape.

Students move about the school, either parallel to the contours on the two main corridors or across the contours, connecting up and down the slope. A given requirement of the Dept of Education & Science is that a school be single-storey. This school, though single-storey, is in fact built on three levels – the upper corridor has classrooms and specialist rooms. The lower corridor has the administration offices and its own specialist rooms. Two ramping spaces join the upper and lower corridors to complete the circuit. The sports hall is placed 1.8m below the lower corridor, part of which acts as a viewing gallery into the sports hall, connecting the largest volume of the building into the everyday experience of the school .

Secondary schools are subject-based, which means that the students move from subject room to subject room throughout the day, from music to mathematics, from physics to physical education. Over the years, the Dept of Education & Science has developed a standard educational layout for each subject room. This means that the design of a secondary school is like a jigsaw puzzle, where the fixed layout plans of subject rooms have to be 'held together' architecturally, physically, educationally and socially.

Classrooms are placed individually in rows at the edge of the plan where they look out to the landscape and the sky, or

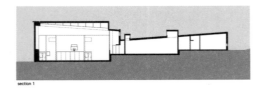

section 1

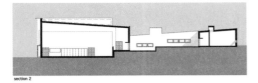

section 2

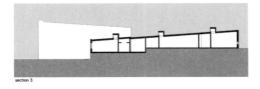

section 3

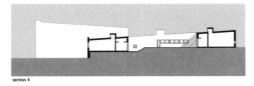

section 4

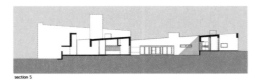

section 5

they are placed in the interior of the plan in pairs, looking into one of the four courtyards. We developed a pattern where specifically sized rooms are locked together into a 19m long matrix, creating a mat or weave of built and unbuilt spaces, perpendicular to the contours. The retaining walls in the foundations stagger across the plan to form a new 'fault line' at the point where rooms accessed from the upper corridor meet rooms which are accessed off the lower corridor. The 'lightboxes' placed at the roof level follow this 'fault line'. The form of the roof reflects the form of the new floor plate of the school, and in itself forms new ground. The spaces of the school are formed between these two plates.

There are over sixty rooms of varying sizes in this school. The main accommodation includes ten general classrooms, two inter-connecting classrooms, library, tiered lecture room, religion and meditation area, mathematics room, language laboratory, three science laboratories, two home economics rooms, dress-design room, art and craft room, technology and computer rooms, music and drama rooms, social studies and guidance rooms, general purpose area with kitchenette, a 608m^2 sports hall and changing rooms.

The open-ended nature of the plan allows a hierarchy of entrances and exits, which rationalise the movement of the 450 students within this 4,141m^2 school. The main entrance, facing the avenue, is reached by a series of steps and ramps. The south-facing gable of the sports hall plays a role in this entrance sequence. It acts as a 'deflector' on the route to the entrance canopy/wind shield, which then leads into the reception area and the general-purpose area, placed at the heart of the school, which opens on to one of the

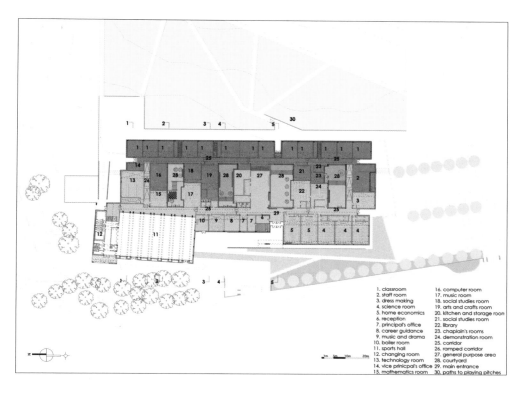

1. classroom
2. staff room
3. dress making
4. science room
5. home economics
6. reception
7. principal's office
8. career guidance
9. music and drama
10. boiler room
11. sports hall
12. changing room
13. technology room
14. vice prinicpal's office
15. mathematics room
16. computer room
17. music room
18. social studies room
19. arts and crafts room
20. kitchen and storage room
21. social studies room
22. library
23. chaplain's rooms
24. demonstration room
25. corridor
26. ramped corridor
27. general purpose area
28. courtyard
29. main entrance
30. paths to playing pitches

four open-air courtyards. Close to this main entrance a group of mature trees has been retained. The scale of the trees acts to 'absorb' the mass of the sports hall. A separate route through these trees to its own entrance allows the sports hall to be used independently from the rest of the school. Changing facilities associated with the sports hall are positioned to allow immediate access to the five basketball courts, grass pitches and landscaped areas. The staff room, with its own south-facing terrace, is strategically positioned to oversee the two south entrances and to be close to the parking area. The vice principal's office is positioned to monitor the entrance close by. The only entrance/exit to the east allows the students access to the landscaped areas.

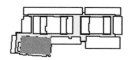

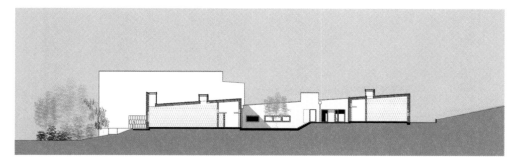

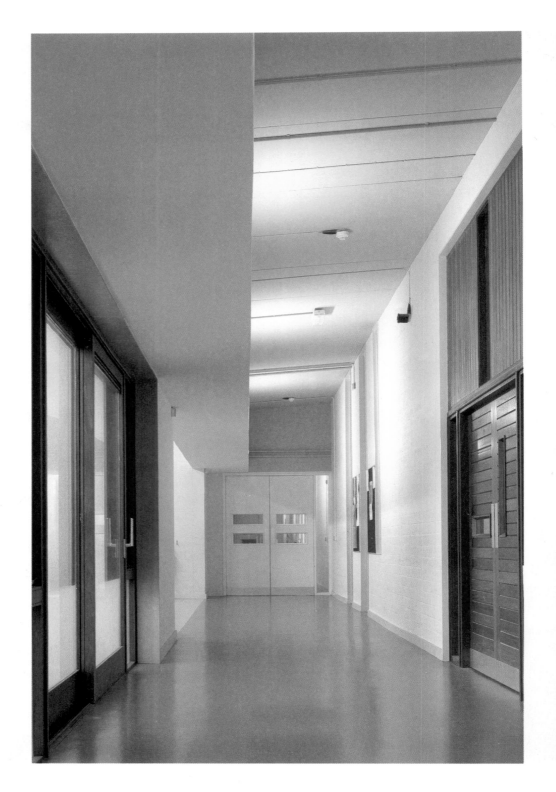

1

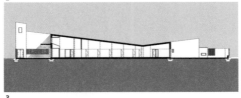

2

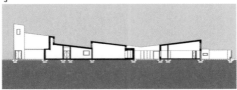

3

5

6

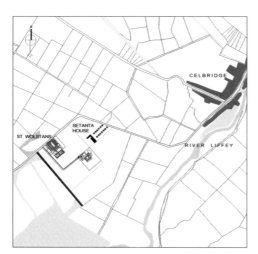

NORTH KILDARE EDUCATE TOGETHER

In primary schools, children are based in one classroom for the academic year. Each of the classrooms in this school enjoys a democracy of orientation, capturing the pattern of the sun throughout the seasons, and has its own garden. Each child occupies a studio/workshop/classroom, with its own small-scale versatile 'den' acting as a stage or a retreat for quiet reading.

The idea was to bring the original meadow into the experience of the new school. The plan is a series of courtyards, the centrifugal force of the main courtyard anchoring the ten classrooms with their own 'private' courtyards. Over time, flowers, plants, trees, bird and insect life will reclaim these newly built spaces. The main courtyard is designed to become a sensory garden – the secret garden at the heart of the school.

Set on the flat landscape of Co Kildare, the ground plane of this school is on one level, with the undulating roofscape changing the volumes and character of the rooms below, and the lightboxes changing the quality of light. Natural materials – red brick, iroko timber windows, terracotta window sills, birch plywood wall panelling, and copper-coated roof – are used to enrich the tactile experience of the school.

In its isolated location, layers of protection are required, both for the site and for the building itself. The arrival area is monitored by the reception, the principal's office, the staff room and the library. Adjacent to the entrance hall is the school office, the general-purpose hall, the multi-purpose/servery area, and the two classrooms for the youngest students. The rest of the school is accessed by a corridor, which wraps around the central courtyard.

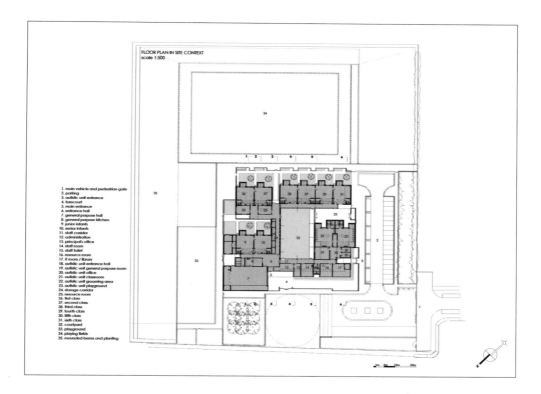

FLOOR PLAN IN SITE CONTEXT
scale 1:500

1. main vehicle and pedestrian gate
2. parking
3. autistic unit entrance
4. forecourt
5. main entrance
6. entrance hall
7. general purpose hall
8. general purpose kitchen
9. junior infants
10. senior infants
11. staff corridor
12. administration
13. principal's office
14. staff room
15. staff toilet
16. resource room
17. it room / library
18. autistic unit entrance hall
19. autistic unit general purpose room
20. autistic unit office
21. autistic unit classroom
22. autistic unit grooming area
23. autistic unit playground
24. storage corridor
25. resource room
26. first class
27. second class
28. third class
29. fourth class
30. fifth class
31. sixth class
32. courtyard
33. playground
34. playing fields
35. mounded berms and planting

The main all-weather outdoor play area is positioned to benefit from the morning sun. A grass pitch is proposed to the south. Mounds are formed to screen the edges of the site and to connect to the mountains and the sky. Nature walks are planned for the future.

The integration of the children with autism was fundamental to the ethos of this school. Both of the studio/ workshop/classrooms have the versatile 'den' that all the other classrooms in the school have, as well as special study carrels which allow for the focus of each individual, a dedicated play corner and a changing area. The all-weather play area, with its outdoor toys store, connects these two classrooms directly into the central courtyard/sensory garden. As well as the main school entrance, there is another entrance, accessed directly from the car park. This allows for independent arrival into an entrance area, with its own general-purpose room, ancillary and relaxation rooms. The library and resource room are positioned so that they can be used both as an integral part of the school and independently after school hours.

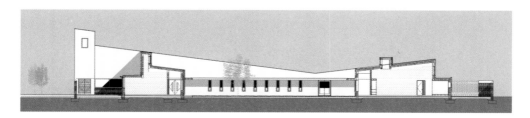

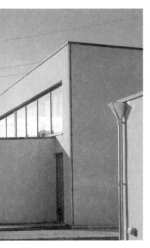

ASSESSORS' COMMENTS

BETSKY – Here in the secondary school [Ballinasloe] you actually see what the small windows do. I think with very minimal means there's some really beautiful things in that interior. And it has sophistications. Like, it's a very simple corridor plan – you enter here and you don't enter exactly into that [circulation] space, you come around and there's the space, you just have enough of an angle here to create a little bit more room for this bigger space. I must say I think this one's more complex and slightly more sophisticated than the primary school [Celbridge].

CONROY – The secondary school is a much more sophisticated project. But I think they are both very clear – the iconography of the entrance element, and the use of the concrete technology to make those indirect rooflights and bigger spans. It's all very carefully done.

BETSKY – This looks like it's been such a triumph against the odds, wresting a great deal of spatial variety, attention to scale, sequence and detailing from very minimal means. I'm impressed by the sensitive planning, which seems to respond in great detail to the way the spaces are used and experienced, and by the beautiful compositions using very rough and simple materials.

O'NEILL – It probably was a triumph against the odds, given the constraints of Dept of Education budgets, and we have seen other examples of this. I really love this image of how light enters the classrooms in Ballinasloe. Its all about the roof and how it mediates the light.

ROBBRECHT – Yes, it's terrific. It's beautiful. These are well-thought-out rational plans for schools, economically organised.

CONROY – And Ballinasloe commands the space in front of it very, very calmly. I think it's a beautiful building.

ROBBRECHT – And both of these strictly organised schemes have, at the same time, very variable appearances, organised around courtyards or communicating with the surrounding landscape. And they have well-proportioned and empathic inner spaces.

FINUCANE – With a joint project, do we distinguish between the two? Personally I would prefer the secondary school to the primary school.

CONROY – Celbridge is nothing like as complex as Ballinasloe, and I don't think it is quite as clever, and the courtyard arrangement isn't as convincing.

BETSKY – The [Celbridge] courtyard looks okay there in that photograph. But the exterior is not as good as the other project.

CONROY – They both have very controlled readings on the outside. You know the way sometimes these schools are agglomerations of things, and somehow here they've all been turned into a positive reading about the whole.

O'NEILL – And externally Ballinasloe refers very well to the landscape. Both of them work well within their contexts.

BETSKY – Yes. This is the way to do it. If you're going to play with form, this is how you play. If you want to play with light, this is how you play.

FINUCANE – Some of the classrooms look a bit small on the plans, but then I suppose that's to do with the tight Dept of Education budget and brief.

ROBBRECHT – My preference is for that one [Ballinasloe], but both of them are of very high quality. The strange thing is that I feel the light, the possible life in this building [Ballinasloe] ... It can be occupied by people, by children... And also I think I have the feeling that it is very beautifully situated in the landscape. But both of them are very beautiful.

CONROY – It's an award.

BETSKY – Oh yes, without a doubt. I think it's a question of whether this joint project gets the medal or not. Of everything we've seen today, I think this is the best.

O'NEILL – It's really very good, very well considered.

FINUCANE – The pair of schools is one of the projects that jumped out at me from the very beginning.

ROBBRECHT – This [Ballinasloe] is a really beautiful building, it's authentic. If I come here as a foreigner, this is for me an Irish project that I really hardly would find in another country. That makes it so strong for me.

CONROY – I must say, I'm very pleased that the school has won, because everybody thinks it's impossible to build a good school. And now it has the Downes Medal on a Dept of Education budget. It will push everybody; it will lift the whole game.

GRAFTON ARCHITECTS – established in 1977. Shelley McNamara and Yvonne Farrell graduated from University College Dublin in 1974. Fellows of the RIAI. Founder members of Group 91 Architects. Studio lecturers at the School of Architecture, UCD, and visiting critics to schools of architecture abroad. Winners of AAI Awards in 1993, 1995, 1997, 1998, 2000, 2002, and 2003. Work exhibited in Ireland and abroad, including the RIAI Exhibition Centre (1999), Venice Biennale (2002), Mies van der Rohe Award Exhibition (2003). Work widely published, including *Architecture Profile 3 – Grafton Architects* (Gandon Editions, 1999). Winners of international competition for Luigi Bocconi University in Milan. Associate and project directors: Gerard Carty, Philippe O'Sullivan, Emmett Scanlon.

ASST ARCHITECTS FOR BALLINASLOE – Iseult Hall, Michael Pike, Philip Comerford, Aoibheann Ní Mhearainn, Ansgar Staudt, Martin McKenna, Matthew Beattie, Miriam Dunn

ASST ARCHITECTS FOR CELBRIDGE – Michael Pike, Ansgar Staudt, Anna Ryan

GRAFTON ARCHITECTS
12 Dame Court, Dublin 2
T 01-6713365 / F 01-6713178 /
E info@graftonarchitects.ie

CIGAR BOX, North Great George's Street, Dublin

DENIS BYRNE ARCHITECTS

The L-shaped site occupies part of a 'corner' in the conservation areas of the north-inner-city Georgian grid, between a Victorian warehouse and a pastiche Georgian apartment development. The building strategy chosen emphasises the border nature of the site, and aims to differentiate between the buildings on the corner and the Georgian terraces. This is achieved by inserting on the site a new space analogous to a lane or side street. The new building 'bookends' the existing buildings that reach back from the Parnell Street corner.

The building, thus separated from the Georgian discipline, was free to look to the adjoining warehouse building, and elsewhere, for clues as to how to build. Clues provided were the size and proportion of door and window openings, floor-to-floor heights, and general 'feel'. The building was intended to be unpretentious and direct, qualities associated with warehouse buildings. The materials used are traditional – brick, stone, timber, glass and metal – all used in a straightforward way.

The main entrance and staircase (with dumb waiter) are found in the new space between the buildings. This space is covered by a glass roof above timber-slatted under-lining, but is otherwise open to the elements. The red-stained timber lining continues down against the existing gable wall to enclose the staircase. This entrance space is intensely and celebratory urban in experience. As one ascends the staircase, views of

Georgian Dublin appear and alternate with the Rotunda's spire. In the afternoon, sunlight pours through here.

The large apartments, one per floor, are shaped to maximise available light on a tight site. Each one is entered from the access deck through a private west-facing balcony. The apartments contain an oak-lined entrance lobby (the 'cigar-box'), but are otherwise open loft-type spaces, with painted concrete block walls and concrete ceilings. Oak floors and oak wall-linings soften this sparse robustness. Bedroom and kitchen balconies and large external double doors in the main living space enrich the restrained interiors. The open spaces allow flexibility of bedroom sizes and numbers. The two offices, front and back, each occupy a part of the ground and basement floors, and are both lit by the central light-well and front and round-the-corner rear windows. Finishes here continue the warehouse feel.

This simple building with its covered side space has two ambitions – to extend the vocabulary of the city, and to provide a good example of contemporary architecture in a historic context.

Location – 26 North Great George's Street, Dublin 1.
Area – 565m². Stage – completed Autumn 2003.

bottom
Plans (basement, ground floor, 1st, 2nd, 3rd, 4th)

opposite
Elevation to North Great George's Street
Section through terrace
Cross-section through staircase

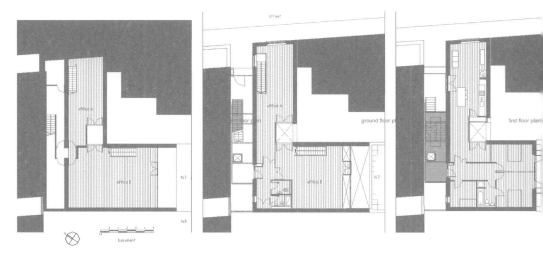

No.27A   No.27   No.26   No.25

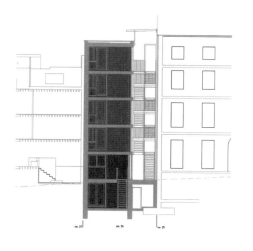

no.27   no.26   no.25

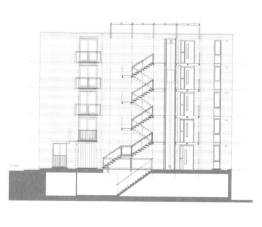

street

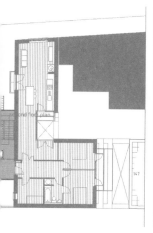

second floor plan

147

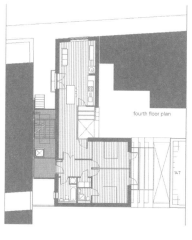

fourth floor plan

147

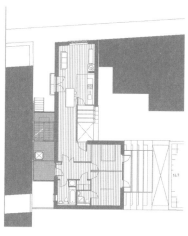

147

ASSESSORS' COMMENTS

ROBBRECHT – I like this project. It is an intelligent use of a restricted piece of land in its Georgian Dublin context. And an interesting typology has been given to the apartments themselves.

O'NEILL – I like the way it slips behind the buildings, the way it deals with where it is. It's in a very specific place without resorting to pastiche. This is a very powerful street coming down to it, very powerful Georgian architecture, and then it has the warehouse building on the other side of it. I just think it's a very, very strong project externally.

CONROY – I think the slot achieves an incredible amount. On the one hand, it mediates between the Victorian and the Georgian blocks. And then the steel stairways become interesting places. So the slot becomes a kind of presence rather than an absence. I think it's characterful, with the timber travelling up the stair sides and turning over the top. And then this idea of the timber box, the 'cigar box', that travels up through it...

BETSKY – What do you mean by 'travels up through it'? There's just a bathroom box clad in wood on every floor.

CONROY – Yes, but you can see it right up through the building, particularly at night when it's lit. The site looks tight on the plans, but as the building steps up, the floor plans get smaller to allow light to travel down. It's very careful about the exact distances between things. It's an almost impossible site, but it has made just the right gestures to deal with a Georgian condition, a Victorian condition, and offer light-filled, good-quality apartments.

FINUCANE – I agree with you about its light-filled quality, but I really don't like the façade in this Georgian street. I really do like the light-filled interiors, and I like the way the plan works on a very tight site. But I really don't like that façade.

BETSKY – I just see a building that seems an arbitrary height, higher than the building next to it, with no gesture made to accept that, and that tries to make a relationship with its neighbour by abstracting it, but because it is set forward and then stuck on to it, it doesn't have the presence that can allow it to answer back. So, it seems to me that it's neither fish nor fowl. And then I look at the spaces that are made, and I see kind of L-form spaces which don't seem to have a centre or focus or any kind of presence, where you have to sort of slide by the sideboard or the table there. I don't quite understand how these spaces are actually used.

FINUCANE – I really like the interior spaces. I would live there with all that. I just wonder about the façade.

BETSKY – But the fire escape is just a fire escape. It's not a place to hang out. It's a fire escape. This isn't West Side Story.

CONROY – A staircase like this is an unusual gesture here [in Dublin], where it isn't that common. But I think that there's a lot more made out of it, in design terms, than what might have been.

O'NEILL – Yes. I like the activity on the side. The hoist and vertical circulation are successful on the street. When you come to the end of the street they deal with the

transition from existing buildings to contemporary. But I'm not convinced about the inside spaces.

O'NEILL – Those images of the kitchen and living area are kind of clumsy and chunky. And I don't think there's anything special about the fenestration there.

BETSKY – Think what that interior would have been like if it had gotten the minimal treatment of some of those expensive house additions we saw earlier. It would have been so much more successful.

ROBBRECHT – I like the plan and I like the façade, I really do. It has this kind of autonomy, holding its place there in the street. The staircase might be indulgent – but there's no elevator, no? The project uses a very tiny place in a very rich way, the way the apartments are just put in-between these two walls. The windows there relate to this Georgian house, on the one hand, but on the other hand it's quite an autonomous thing. If you look further along the street elevation, you see that it [the parapet height] jumps up again, so it works.

CONROY – I think it's very careful about stepping back for light. The stairs, as well, is a kind of an adventure in Dublin. It's not typical, but very urban.

ROBBRECHT – Yes. That's probably very much inspired by that scheme in Basel, with the wavy metal façade.

BETSKY – And what does it look like at the rear? We never get to see it. Considerably more massive, I would suspect.

ROBBRECHT – I like this project. I think it is a very good urban intervention.

DENIS BYRNE – graduated from University College Dublin in 1982 and moved to London to live and work. There he formed a partnership with Brian Beardsmore and Simon Yauner before returning to Dublin in 1991. After working with the National Building Agency and Richard Hurley, amongst others, he formed Denis Byrne Architects in 2000. The winner of previous AAI and RIAI awards, he was studio tutor at DIT from 1993 to 2003, where he is currently a visiting critic.

DESIGN TEAM – Roland Bosbach, Denis Byrne, Nadina Castelli, Dave English, Giuliano Mignemi

DENIS BYRNE ARCHITECTS
26 North Great George's Street, Dublin 1
T 01-8788535 / F 01-87884738
E info@architects-dba.com
W www.architects-dba.com

UTILITY BUILDING, Clontarf, Dublin

DE PAOR ARCHITECTS

As part of a programme of public space design initiatives for Dublin City Council (in association with the Royal Institute of Architects of Ireland), a phased programme of works was
developed to reinforce and amplify the existing amenity of the village centre at the junction of Vernon Avenue and the Clontarf Road on Dublin's northern coastline. The works
include the rationalisation of all short-term parking in the village by the material remodelling of the street edges, installing new street furniture and public lighting, and developing
a planted and lit seaside ground plane as esplanade, on which cars park, protected from
occasional high tides by a 1.2m high, 240m long earthwork to replace an existing defence
wall and unify the landscape.

The first phase required redeveloping an existing pump station as part of Dublin
City Council Waste Water Division's environmental upgrades to Dublin Bay, with the provi-
sion for a maintenance depot for the City Council Parks Department and an ESB substation. The dilapidated structure was removed above ground while maintaining all pump
operations below. A new folded plate superstructure of reinforced concrete, forming an
interlock of canted walls and roof slabs, was poured onto the extended existing concrete

61

two-storey basement.The relationship between the restored maintenance crane and the below-ground pumps was maintained.

The new volume rotates visually across the reclaimed ground to catch the light and open relationships with the Clontarf Road, the village, the sea wall, and the docklands beyond the estuary. This massing intimates the internal complexity of the tripartite programme, but within the presence of a single object. A closed public building, each façade opens alternately to pump station, park depot or electrical substation, each autonomous, but linked spatially by a shared requirement for natural ventilation in a folded slot of space which incorporates the requirements for separate toilet and shower facilities and water tank. The diesel back-up generator ventilation is expressed directly to the east below a fixed glazed clerestory to the pump monitors – the only requirement for daylight. All internal services are face-fixed to the shot-blasted concrete, except for a pair of tea stations that are cast into the structure. All internal grilles are stainless steel.

The structure and access doors are dressed in a prepatinated copper-shingle rain screen to envelope the form as a continuous wrapping. It is punctured twice by the ventilation slot, which is expressed in untreated iroko louvres and will weather grey. On each exposure this patination will develop differently to exaggerate the modelling of the enclosure. This skin is eroded to the east, allowing the gathered rain waters to discharge over and stain the shot-blasted concrete.

Location – Vernon Avenue, Clontarf, Dublin 3.
Area – 158m² (above ground). Stage – phase 1 completed November 2003.

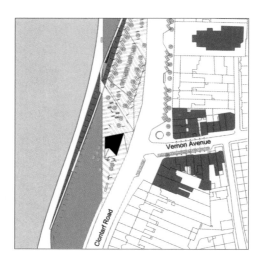

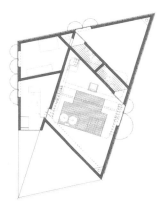

PLAN +1000

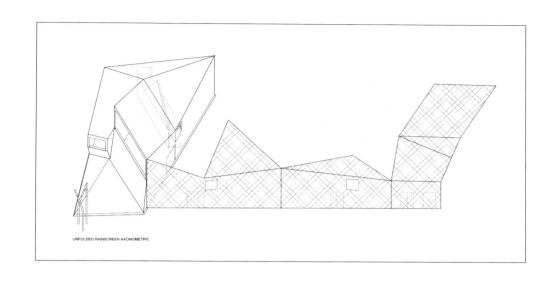

UNFOLDED RAINSCREEN AXONOMETRIC

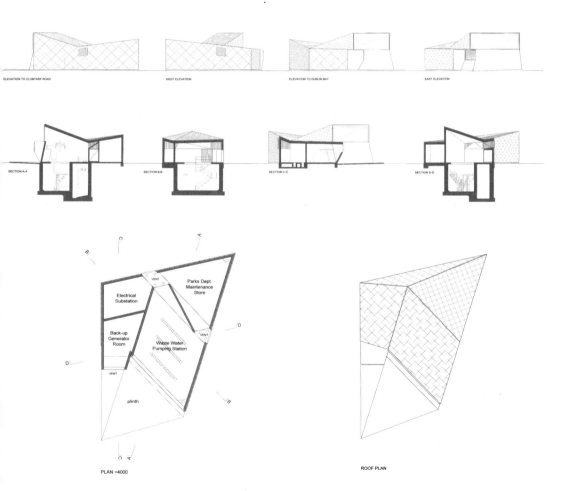

ELEVATION TO CLONTARF ROAD

WEST ELEVATION

ELEVATION TO DUBLIN BAY

EAST ELEVATION

SECTION A-A

SECTION B-B

SECTION C-C

SECTION D-D

Parks Dept.
Maintenance
Store

Electrical
Substation

Back-up
Generator
Room

Waste Water
Pumping Station

VENT

plinth

PLAN +4000

ROOF PLAN

ASSESSORS' COMMENTS

O'NEILL – I really love the cladding – it's almost like skin or scales.

BETSKY – What does that big window do? All that big window is doing, is lighting this pumping station, and no-one gets to see that space.

O'NEILL – Well not from the inside. The building is not used by the public.

CONROY – I presume it has a night reading, it glows at night.

O'NEILL – Yes, at night it's very dramatic. It faces down along the esplanade by the sea; in that way it is very public, like a piece of public art.

ROBBRECHT – I know this building! Coming in from from the airport, I passed by it. It's like a sculptural object in a long park. This building has remarkable volumetrics that brighten-up a walk in the park or a journey to the airport.

CONROY – I think it's interesting that something this prosaic would be given so gnomic or arcane a language. The only thing I don't like is the way the rain-screen stops along the concrete wall. It just stops, rather than being detailed to a halt. But I think it's very interesting formally.

O'NEILL – And I really think it's a pity about the [ventilation] louvre, because I like the way the light plays on the diagonal cladding.

ROBBRECHT – Yes, the louvre is unfortunate. It doesn't make sense the way it is done.

CONROY – It's very unusual to be able to dramatise such a small, prosaic object. It animates the space around it.

BETSKY – All over the world it's becoming more and more a fashion now. More and more utility companies are hiring architects for such buildings.

FINUCANE – So they're not hiding things like pumping stations as much.

BETSKY – I find there's no relationship to function. I don't quite understand its relationship with the street. The big move of the window seems to have absolutely no relationship with the interior or with the exterior. It's just sort of an almost.

FINUCANE – I really like it. And it adjusts people's heads to the notion that architecture is not just about rich people with money, big corporations, or big public buildings.

CONROY – That's what's good about it.

BETSKY – It is a piece of urban infrastructure on which some care has been lavished, and that participates now in the life of the city.

TOM DE PAOR – born in 1967. Studied architecture at DIT Bolton Street and at UCD, graduating in 1991. He is currently year master at UCD, and teaching at the AA in London. De Paor Architects has won several AAI and RIAI awards.
DESIGN TEAM – A Cocherane, T de Paor, T Maher (project architect), K Smith (project architect)

DE PAOR ARCHITECTS
12 Mountjoy Parade, Dublin 1
T 01-8349599 / F 01-8349600 / E office@depaor.com

BRICK HOUSE, Milltown Path, Dublin 6

FKL ARCHITECTS

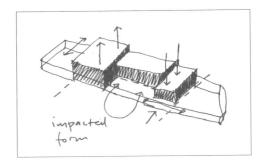

The site for this house in the centre of an Edwardian block near Palmerston Park is a leftover plot slotted in behind the extensive gardens of the area, which are defined by their red-brick walls and quite removed from the surrounding protected structures. The site is extreme at 53m long by 8.3m wide, with access by car from a lane at one narrow end, and by foot from the client's family home at the other.

The concept of the house was dictated by the site, the brief requirements, and the inevitable choice of brick as the main building material, giving a materiality capable of determining the image of the house – a massive solid, impacted upon by restrictions on scale and height and the need to minimise the impact on its genteel surroundings. Sliding windows are set flush with the brickwork to reinforce the reading of the form, and are placed to give a reserved relationship between the house and the external spaces – a contemporary interpretation of the formal relationship between the surrounding houses and their gardens.

Internal spaces are simple expressions of the external form, establishing a spatial dynamic between the stepping of the site and the stepping of the form. This reinforces the clear sequence from entry to living room, terminating with the view back through the dinning area. Extensive rooflighting floods the centre of the plan with light and establishes a relationship with surrounding trees and the sky as a distant view.

Overlooked on all sides, the roof has been treated as a non-Corbusian 'fifth elevation', with a flush brick parapet blending with the colour-matched paving slab to give a seamless and homogeneous appearance when viewed from the surrounding houses. This imbues the house with an abstract quality, which places the roofscape in the realm of an uninhabited landscape or folly, particularly when seen emerging above the surrounding garden walls and partially obscured by the trees.

Area – 185m². Stage – completed Nov 2003.

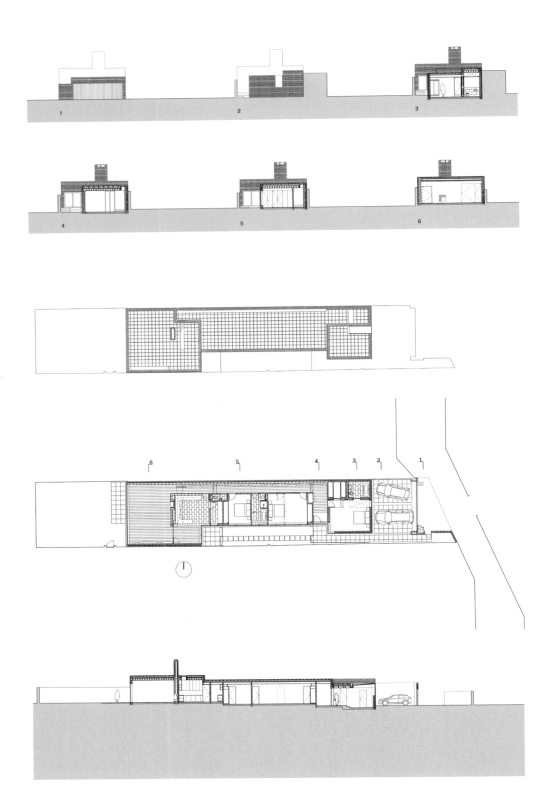

ASSESSORS' COMMENTS

ROBBRECHT – It is a very clear scheme, with a strong sense of materials, embedded in the context of Edwardian housing and gardens.

BETSKY – Yes, it's a very tight site.

ROBBRECHT – A very tight site in the opposite direction to everything else around it. So, it's like one piece of land that is not existing. Then I like the plan. It's not a completely original plan, but it's quite interesting.

BETSKY – What is interesting about it?

ROBBRECHT – For instance, there is no more land than this.

BETSKY – Right, and you have to set-back on one side.

ROBBRECHT – And you have really closed things. It's possible to have different kinds of walks in this house. Inside, you can walk along here, or all the way along there.

CONROY – The one thing that I was surprised at was they didn't take the kitchen along there, which would have let you in earlier.

ROBBRECHT – And then there's the use of materials.

CONROY – This brick roof is dare-devil detailing. Look at the roof! The glass goes up vertically and then flat across. It's high-risk detailing.

BETSKY – I thought it was a modestly elegant effort, and I really like that façade. But it seems confused as to whether it is a courtyard house or a row house, and it is neither, nor. And by trying to have, as you say, that choice [of circulation], as far as I can tell what you wind up with are some very tight spaces.

FINUCANE – But it's an imaginative project on a very awkward site. It really does sit into that backdrop very comfortably

BETSKY – The spaces could have been bigger, if the architect hadn't wanted to have corridors on both sides. These kind of internal rooms, to me, are not all that convincing, and of course, they are not shown with any furniture. What happens to them once they're occupied?

FINUCANE – They didn't want to put you off with a naff chair.

BETSKY – It's a very pleasant house in some ways. In other places, it feels a little uncomfortable.

CONROY – It's very minimal and very clear. It's a cliché that people say a wall is thick enough to become a house, but here it literally is. I like the monolithic nature of it in this genteel backlands setting.

ROBBRECHT – And also the domestic quality.

O'NEILL – Yes, everything is thought about, the way the entrance steps just stop at precisely the correct place. And that image of the courtyard is dense and urban and beautifully put together. It's extremely elegant.

BETSKY – Maybe it's just because I would never live this way, but it seems to me strange to have bedrooms caught in the middle here, with guests walking by, a corridor on the other side, and this big living room undifferentiated at the end. It would seem much more logical, given the site, that you would have the kitchen/living area here, that you have all of the living here with its own courtyard, the core of the bathroom against the garage, and the two bedrooms at the end, looking out on the grounds.

O'NEILL – No. I think the strength of it is that when you get to the end it opens out and gives you as much as it does under the constraints.

ROBBRECHT – You have to imagine it's a family with children, and the children have their own entrance to come and go on the street.

CONROY – Volumetrically it looks more interesting that it does on the plan.

O'NEILL – But everything's considered. The roof's incredible, and the fact they designed it as a fifth elevation and turned the brickwork onto it is an example of this consideration.

FINUCANE – The roof looks great but does it really keep the water out?

CONROY – It's simply paviours with brick eaves and glass inserts. I don't really know how it's possible to do it in Ireland, but...

ROBBRECHT – I would like it for an award.

O'NEILL – We are going to have to invent dense, satisfactory ways of developing sites like this one within the city suburbs, and it has done that. It's tidily tucked in here, unobtrusively.

CONROY – It's a bit mysterious, isn't it?

FINUCANE – It's also an example of a really imaginative solution to a domestic situation.

FKL ARCHITECTS – established in 1998 by Michelle Fagan, Paul Kelly and Gary Lysaght. They graduated from Bolton Street DIT in 1990 / 1989 / 1990. Their work has been published and exhibited in a number of countries, and has received several awards, including AAI Awards.

DESIGN TEAM – Diarmaid Brophy, Michelle Fagan, Paul Kelly, Gary Lysaght, Sterrin O'Shea

FKL ARCHITECTS
31-32 Little Strand Street, Dublin 7
T 01-8779009 / F 01-8779006 / E design@fklarchitects.com
W www.fklarchitects.com

DOUBLE GLASS HOUSE, Dublin

HASSETT DUCATEZ ARCHITECTS

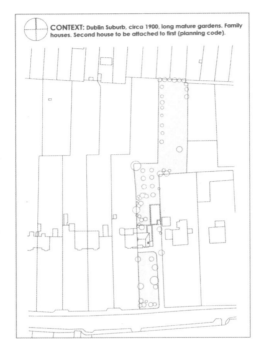

CONTEXT: Dublin Suburb, circa 1900, long mature gardens. Family houses. Second house to be attached to first (planning code).

Two families, grandparents, grandchildren and parents. A large existing mature garden with an old house, *c.*1900. The brief – two new connected glass houses.

Both families agreed to share the long garden. Planning code required the second house remain attached to the old house. The living rooms of the old house face mostly north. The old house was opened up at its side, drawing east and south sunlight into the living rooms. As a consequence, privacy between neighbours was required. Two new glass skins are drawn around the existing house, facing south, east, north and west. As the sunlight tracks around through the day, the glass skin is variously pierced by light, appearing sometimes as solid, sometimes as translucent. Living spaces are arranged to provide partial screening and some sharing of the garden. The two long living spaces can be interconnected by choice through opening mirror doors.

The project was technically demanding, achieving environmental comfort, minimising solar-gain, and providing ventilation, in addition to ensuring a level of privacy and comfort for older and younger members of the family. Air is drawn through holes in the steel plinth beam supporting the weight of the glass. The air is warmed and released through holes in the red merbau floor, and rises to a ceiling vent. The glass is clear blue, white opal laminate, and gold or silver mirror, depending on its performance function or orientation, with a glass-to-glass joint.

At dusk, electric light reveals new interior bodies. Mirror and one-way views dissolve corners and trick the mind. Ten golden mirror glass doors reflect the garden endlessly, playing with perception as they swing open. The domestic interior always enters the realm of the imagination.

Area – 155m². Stage – completed Spring 2003.

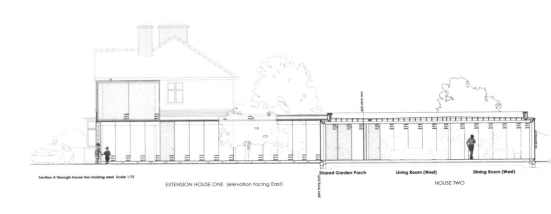

Section A through house two looking west Scale 1:75

EXTENSION HOUSE ONE (elevation facing East)

Shared Garden Porch   Living Room (West)   Dining Room (West)

HOUSE TWO

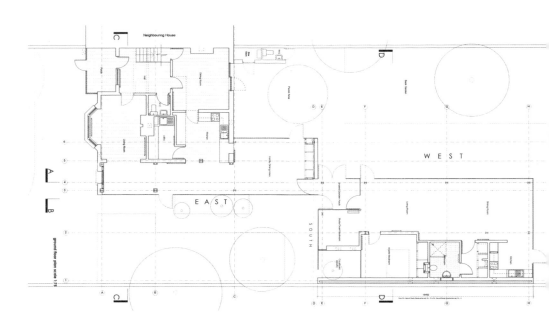

Neighbouring House

WEST

EAST

SOUTH

ground floor plan scale 1:75

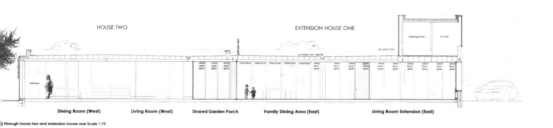

HOUSE TWO   EXTENSION HOUSE ONE

Dining Room (West)   **Living Room (West)**   **Shared Garden Porch**   **Family Dining Area (East)**   **Living Room Extension (East)**

through house two and extension house one Scale 1:75

Section D (facing south) through house two. (rear north elevation existing house)

ASSESSORS' COMMENTS

CONROY – The detailing is critical – the whole project stands or falls on eaves and eaves lines, and details here are very fudgey. But I have to say that these internal images are fantastic, the merbau floor and the line of glass, and the way they all pivot to the garden. It's beautiful.

BETSKY – Yes, and the plan itself is good.

CONROY – The plan is elegant.

O'NEILL – I wasn't so sure about the junction of the two houses in the plan, whether or not they really slip by each other as might have been intended. I know it's not a plan that's trying to work those things out too seriously, but I just wonder about how successful that is.

FINUCANE – It's just absolutely gorgeous. I mean, that glazed living space overlooking the garden is heavenly.

CONROY – It's also very clever about the issues of reflectivity and transparency. It's very sophisticated in that regard.

ROBBRECHT – There are many detailing problems, as Eddie said earlier, but still the idea is good... And I also wonder how it works at the larger scale, how the two houses work being so close together, and how this particular social situation is resolved in reality.

FINUCANE – I think that rather than being about two distinct houses, the project is really about providing a granny flat. But it is a pretty clever and sophisticated way to solve the problem on a tight site.

ROBBRECHT – It is just a simple glass house. Some parts jar a bit, but it's adventurous housing, reflecting a particular family's life.

CONROY – It's the ultimate granny flat, isn't it?

GRÁINNE HASSETT – Born in 1967. Graduated from DIT Bolton Street in 1991. Worked in Paris and Dublin prior to setting up practice, and is currently carrying out research under the Arts Council/OPW Kevin Kieran Award for Architectural Research, awarded in 2003. Hassett Ducatez Architects have received numerous of awards, including AAI Awards in 1996, 2000 and 2001.

DESIGN TEAM – Claire Crowley, Gráinne Hassett, Sarah Jolley, Fiona Martin, Darrell O'Donoghue

HASSETT DUCATEZ ARCHITECTS
65 Great Strand Street, Dublin 1
T 01-8786122 / F 01-8786134
E hassettducatez@eircom.net

TUBBERCURRY LIBRARY AND CIVIC OFFICES

McCULLOUGH MULVIN ARCHITECTS

The Tubbercurry Civic Offices and Library project provides public services for the people of south Co Sligo, and a civic focus for the town of Tubbercurry. It contains local authority area offices, facilities for the health board, a library, and courtroom space for the District Court.

The site is urban-located on Humbert Street, a side street near the town square. It was formerly occupied by houses, two of which were retained in the project. The houses were small and lightly imprinted on the ground, but they had long gardens – luxuriant, overgrown, generous fingers of space – running in plots back from the street.

The project was an opportunity to explore modern concepts of urbanity in a small Irish town. The front façade is directly on the street, and the plan opens back into a series of long, narrow fingers – echoing the original house plots – inviting access deep into the scheme. Activities are placed around the central hall. The library is at one side of the envelope, separated by a glazed screen; offices are at the other. The back of the central hall contains the local council chamber or meeting room, and is visible from the street.

The rectangular plan can be accessed at several places, including a ramp at the side which runs from the car park and is threaded through a narrow throat of space into the lobby. Further routes are set between grids of structure and screens from the front out to the car park at the rear, where their line is visually extended in the paving.

The scheme aims to create a built landscape between two floating planes. The building is covered by a single undulating zinc roof, like the horizon line on the local landscape. It is interrupted by rooflights – large segments cut and folded up, smaller circular lights over the library. The ground floor – with dark limestone paving containing thousands of fossil imprints – is stepped like a piece of open ground, with the floor plate starting at the entrance, folding down in a ramp, and continuing at a lower level to the back door. Two floors of office accommodation are incorporated within the envelope at one side. The main space is fixed by light columns, like tree trunks supporting the roof plane.

Area – 2,500m². Stage – completed 2003.

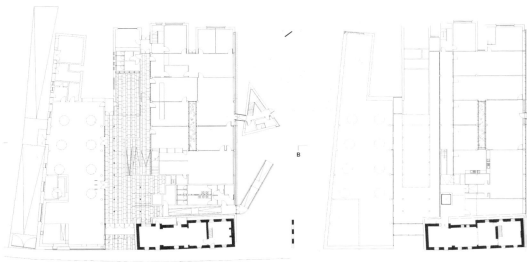

A
B

Main elevation to Humbert Street
Longitudinal section AA
Cross-section BB

opposite
View up Humbert Street from the south
Plans (ground, 1st floor)

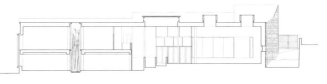

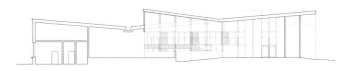

Main entrance
View down Humbert Street, looking south

Main elevation to Humbert Street at night
Rear elevation to the east

overleaf
Atrium, looking towards main entrance, with library on right

ASSESSORS' COMMENTS

BETSKY – This is one of my favourite projects. Although, I must say, every time I think I understand it, I realise I don't quite understand it. I have never quite resolved what the relationship is between the architecture front and back, and the way the central circulation space seems so much larger than it needs to be – I suppose for rhetorical purposes. But I think this is quite a lovely image of a kind of atrium that is a glorified circulation space. I like the façade which is grand and yet completely transparent. It lets you look in. And I think that the planning is quite nice. And I like the way it fits around those two existing houses. But the rear is very hard to judge, because again I can't figure out what the context is, God dammit!

FINUCANE – In the description they talk about mimicking the gardens that had been there originally, like fingers stretching out.

O'NEILL – I'm wondering how you get to the library from the back. When you come from the car park, you come up the ramp to the side door or through a door at the back, but these entrances aren't convincing.

BETSKY – No, no, this is the central atrium space. This is the main circulation space, and you go into the library from there. The cars are back here, so that's just an exit door.

O'NEILL – I think the street presence is great, but the other elevations are not convincing.

CONROY – What's interesting about it, though, is it takes the kind of ordinaryness of an Irish street, and then somehow this grand element transcends it. It's a model for a new public building in a country town. It doesn't need the luxury of a large site outside of town. This nuzzles up beside the buildings adjoining. I think it's an interesting discussion about putting a big building into a town, and adjusting it at the edges.

FINUCANE – That kind of thing is not done very often in a small town. I really like it within the town. I really like it following on from that little terrace.

BETSKY – I think it's very sophisticated. But it's a pity they don't show photographs of it in use. I wish I could see what the inside is really like. This is only an unfurnished shot of the library. It's too bad that we don't see that furnished.

CONROY – That's a very believable image [of the library] with the elliptical rooflights. I think it's beautiful. And the more you look at the central atrium, it has a kind of Asplundian quality.

BETSKY – Yes, very much so. It's all about transition. I love this kind of monumental [wood/glass screen] element. It's so much more sophisticated than some of the other projects in terms of using the preciousness of the wood to play of against the other materials.

ROBBRECHT – It was one of the projects I was generally interested in, but it still doesn't touch me. It's strange, it doesn't touch me at all. And I wonder why. It's a sophisticated building that fits its context along the main street. And it's very refined, with a beautiful use of materials, even in the way the light comes into this atrium space. But I can't believe that there will be life in this space, I don't know why. It is very well done, perhaps it is too well done [pointing to atrium]. But it's very sophisticated.

O'NEILL – I'm not convinced about these finger extensions at the rear.

FINUCANE – That's the weakest part of it really, isn't it?

BETSKY – It breaks down the scale. It makes a monumental façade on the main street, and then starts to break it down towards the parking lot at the rear.

O'NEILL – I'm also not persuaded by the library. There is no sense of it here.

ROBBRECHT – Yes, the library is a problem. Does this building give the reader the opportunity to stay there for a while? I can't feel it. I would not stay here and read my book. It's like reading in a public space. And the rear is questionable. But, I agree that the atrium has a fine quality.

BETSKY – We don't get a sense of the library as a space. But also remember that this is a small community library; it's not a place you would go if you were a scholar. Having the big window to the street, I think, is quite nice. I think that they made a mistake by photographing it without furniture. I think it would probably look a lot more convincing if it was occupied with reading tables and bookshelves. I think these [office areas] will be very nice spaces to occupy as well. That's a really sophisticated building.

O'NEILL – I'm really convinced about it on several levels, and I don't know why, but I've reservations about it. There's something so monumental about the atrium it makes me uneasy. These thin columns that sometimes come from a low wall and sometimes. from the ground... I much prefer the street presence, but looking here I'm just not comfortable with it.

ROBBRECHT – I think at some level that it has to be about people, and that you have such an enormous thing there on the street. I think it's very strange.

McCULLOUGH MULVIN – established in 1985 by Niall McCullough and Valerie Mulvin. Developed particular experience in modern, contextually based architecture of the public realm. Early work included projects for the Abbey Theatre and for the Temple Bar area, where the practice built three urban art and cultural projects. Later work includes the Ussher Library at Trinity College Dublin, which won the Downes Bronze Medal in 2003, the Model Arts & Niland Gallery in Sligo, and civic office complexes in Dun Laoghaire, Donegal and Sligo. Their work has been published as *Work – McCullough Mulvin Architects* (*Anne Street Press / Gandon Editions*, 2004).

McCULLOUGH MULVIN ARCHITECTS
2 Leeson Park, Dublin 6 – T 01-4972266 / F 01-4979592
E macmul@eircom.net / W www.mcculloughmulvin.com

EXTENSION TO VIRUS REFERENCE LABORATORY, University College Dublin

McCULLOUGH MULVIN ARCHITECTS

This extension to the Virus Reference Laboratory was built on a restricted site between the main laboratory and Ardmore House on the upper part of the UCD campus at Belfield. Although small in scale, the project plays a significant role in the relationship between the central university buildings and the surrounding landscape – in particular, the lake directly below it. Quite different in shape and materials, the project is one of a series of new pavilions designed to both support and challenge the ideas of architecture in the landscape that permeated the original campus design in the 1960s.

Designed as a place of work and interchange, with offices on the upper floor and a laboratory, canteen and meeting facility on the ground floor, the pavilion is everywhere concerned with being in landscape and with the interpretation of landscape. It has extensive views to the wider grounds of the university. At a local level, one side is framed by a rational triangular shape on the ground plane. The inner edge is intimately tied around a small Japanese garden.

The plan is simple – open space with a coloured core, like the nucleus of a cell, at one end, which can be glimpsed in the round as one moves around the building. There is also a canted link corridor which connects it back to the main laboratory. Additional height to parapets gives it a cube-like proportional muscularity. The elevations are clad in a skin of abstract interlocking and overlapping shapes in glazing and timber panels, which project and recede from the main surface.

Area – 380m². Stage – completed 2003.

View in context
Site plan
Ground-floor plan

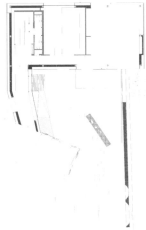

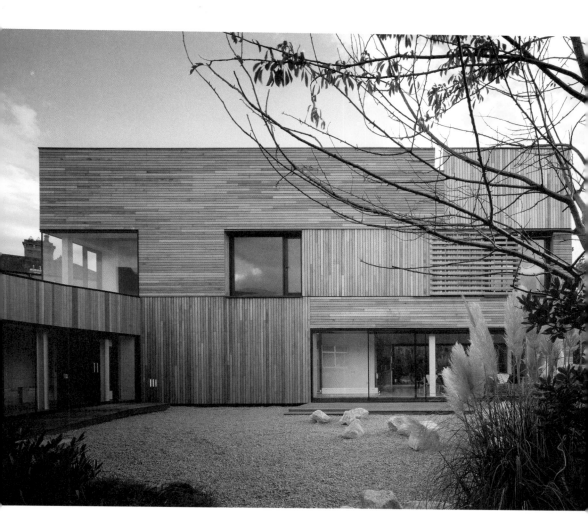

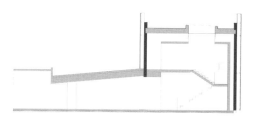

Courtyard
1st floor plan
Section

 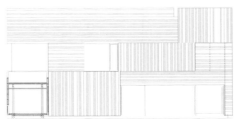

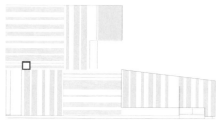

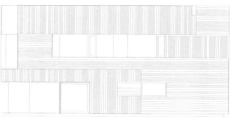

ASSESSORS' COMMENTS

BETSKY – Gorgeous building, but what the hell is going on inside? You're just sort of guessing from this presentation, like, peering into the window.

ROBBRECHT – The one thing they show of the interior, that blue thing there, looks really refined.

CONROY – It sells itself a little bit short in the photographs; it is really lovely. It's centred on a kind of Scandinavian courtyard, like a little oasis in the concrete vastness of Belfield.

FINUCANE – It's a lovely looking building.

ROBBRECHT – I get the impression that the detail and the detailing is really very refined. And in terms of its relationship to the slope of land, and the placing of the box... And the way it levers a little bit there...

CONROY – And this is very gentle – the datum line is created by the slabbing, and the timber box rising up. It's very elegant.

BETSKY – But what the hell is going on inside?

CONROY – Inside it's just laboratories with the stairs at the back.

BETSKY – It's a very, very refined object, but it drives me absolutely batty that they do not show us what context it's existing in. Even in the description, they have this whole thing about how it's so right for its context, and then they don't show the context, not even in drawings.

ROBBRECHT – Just for the refined façade I really would give it an award.

CONROY – Yes, it's very beautiful, isn't it, with its Zen garden. It's very sophisticated.

BETSKY – But if you try and give it anything more, I will fight you. Because the context isn't shown, and the inside isn't shown either. It's basically a nice wrapper, a beautiful wrapper.

FINUCANE – The building exterior is very well done. The only thing is that it's very hard to imagine that it's not as well done inside. But, however, they didn't show it.

BETSKY – I know a lot of architects who make beautiful outsides and throw away the insides.

ROBBRECHT – That's true. But this is a beautifully proportioned object. It must be a happy place in which to work and learn.

McCULLOUGH MULVIN – established in 1985 by Niall McCullough and Valerie Mulvin. Developed particular experience in modern, contextually based architecture of the public realm. Early work included projects for the Abbey Theatre and for the Temple Bar area, where the practice built three urban art and cultural projects. Later work includes the Ussher Library at Trinity College Dublin, which won the Downes Bronze Medal in 2003, the Model Arts & Niland Gallery in Sligo, and civic office complexes in Dun Laoghaire, Donegal and Sligo. Their work has been published as Work – McCullough Mulvin Architects (Anne Street Press / Gandon Editions, 2004).

McCULLOUGH MULVIN ARCHITECTS
2 Leeson Park, Dublin 6 – T 01-4972266 / F 01-4979592
E macmul@eircom.net / W www.mcculloughmulvin.com

MEDICAL RESEARCH LABORATORIES,
University College Dublin

O'DONNELL + TUOMEY ARCHITECTS

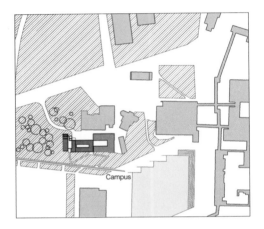

The brief for the new Medical Research Laboratories at University College Dublin's Belfield campus comprised two distinct functions – a research institute for highly specialised investigations in medical microbiology, and laboratories for the routine testing of medical samples. The separate activities share technical resources. The site, on sloping ground among mature trees, is a sheltered location in the campus, on a main pedestrian axis between the entrance car park and bus stop, and the central formal lake.

Single-storey laboratories are planned around a landscaped courtyard and connected to an existing testing facility. Service access is segregated in a delivery yard at the opposite side of the building from staff and visitor entrances. The building is planned to maintain the existing trees, which give a special character to this part of the campus.

The research laboratories are raised above the ground, like north-facing studios, with long views over Dublin Bay. A central stair hall provides a social space between laboratories and offices. Extract fumes are filtered and exhausted via the high chimney roof form, with no pipes on the skyline. The steel-frame structure is clad all over in fibre cement panels, with wooden canteen and conference rooms grouped under the main body of the building.

The brief is specific to the particular functions of research and testing, and the building contains a number of separate dedicated laboratory suites. However, despite the requirements for segregation, the structure had to be designed to accommodate envisaged changes of equipment, technology and function, and the potential for future extension to the west. This requirement for flexibility is reflected in the structural, services and access systems of the building.

A complex brief, stringent technical criteria, restricted budget, and the requirement for clear spaces for concentrated work are resolved in a simple and expressive architectural form, which is the first building visible from the main entrance to the college.

Area – 1,300m². Stage – completed February 2003.

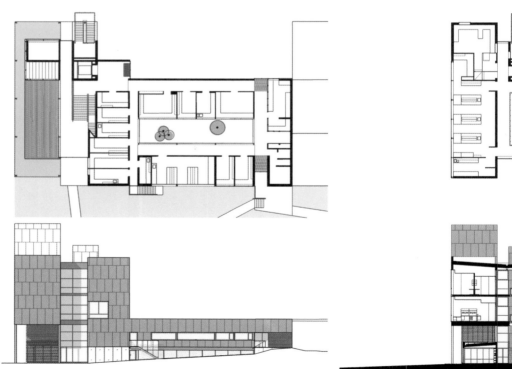

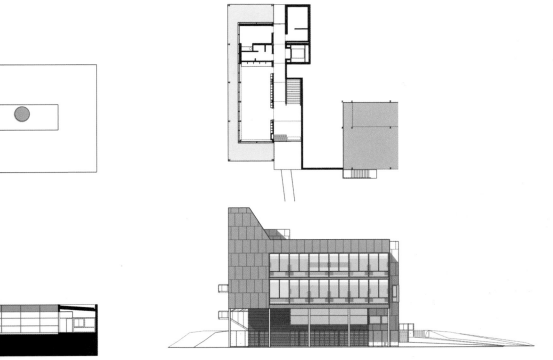

ASSESSORS' COMMENTS

BETSKY – This is the kind of building I would love to be able to visit. It has such a terrific set of images, but does it really work? How does it sit on its site? It's a beautiful composition.

ROBBRECHT – If you look at the plans, it's a very mature piece of architecture. It's true, these photographs present a very strong image. But I consider this as a very strong building, one of the really good projects.

O'NEILL – Yes, it's really strong. I think it's beautiful.

CONROY – I think it's a very strong project.

ROBBRECHT – Also, the materialisation of the cladding, the way it is detailed, is very impressive.

O'NEILL – There's a maturity about the planning which translates all the way down to those images of how it's put together. It's just all so well considered. I like the image at night-time; it's very powerful.

BETSKY – But what really goes on over there [in the undercroft]? I mean, I agree with all of you on its architectural quality, I was immediately taken with it. But the more I look at it, the more I start wondering what goes on in that very high undercroft and in that hollow.

CONROY – This little timber piece passes in underneath that space overhead. There's a lot of bravura sculpting going on there.

BETSKY – But what goes on there, and what does it look like up close?

ROBBRECHT – Maybe it is lifted up to make a statement, to create a landmark at the entrance to the campus. I have real confidence in this quite beautiful building. Look at the plan and the section, and the way these interesting, mature plans are realised in sophisticated volumetrics.

O'NEILL – Yes. And it's also a serious building.

FINUCANE – I really like the west elevation, and I love the plan. I also like the way it sits in among the trees. Now, a certain amount is due to photography, but it's also down to the building.

BETSKY – But, I am puzzled by some things. Where is that upper-ground testing laboratory? Where is that? Where is that whole building? All we see is the tower. And if they

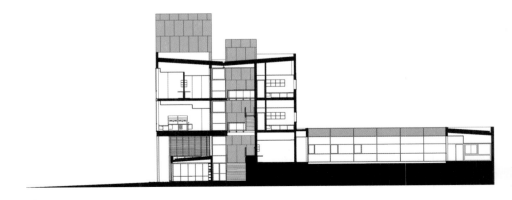

claim it's about the context, why do they never show the full context? Even the model doesn't show the context. I agree with everyone – it's a beautiful object. But I'm really suspicious about what happens there [in the undercroft], and what that [timber screen] really is about. Maybe it's all fine. I mean, it's a very compelling set of images.

O'NEILL – I think this building would be really impressive if we went to visit it. I think that it doesn't describe itself and its particular context in the campus quite as well as it might.

FINUCANE – That makes a great argument for going to visit all the buildings shortlisted for an award.

CONROY – It's very impressive in the photographs.

BETSKY – I am very seduced by this as an object. Some of you have seen it in reality ? So I'm trusting the local assessors that this really works in context as well as it looks here. Because from the photographs – and I really want that to go on record – it is incredibly annoying that they don't show us the relationship to the surrounding buildings.

ROBBRECHT – It is still, for me, a very strong and sophisticated building, one of the really good projects here.

O'DONNELL + TUOMEY – founded in 1988 by Sheila O'Donnell and John Tuomey. The practice has developed an international reputation for cultural and educational buildings, including the Irish Film Centre, the National Photography Centre, and Ranelagh Multi-Denominational School. Currently engaged in the design of university buildings, schools, housing and mixed-use buildings in Ireland and the Netherlands. Urban design projects include the Temple Bar regeneration in Dublin and the Zuid Poort master plan in Delft. Both partners are studio lecturers at UCD, and have taught at schools of architecture in the UK and USA. The work of the practice has been widely published (including an *Architecture Profile* from Gandon Editions) and widely exhibited, and has received many national and international awards, including the AAI Downes Medal in 1988/90/92/97/99 and 2002.

O'DONNELL + TUOMEY ARCHITECTS
20a Camden Row, Dublin 8
T 01-4752500 / F 01-4751479
E info@odonnell-tuomey.ie
W www.odonnell-tuomey.ie

BRICK COURTS HOUSE, 37 Daniel St, Dublin 8

ARCHITECTS BATES MAHER

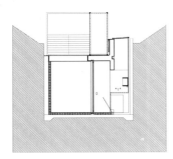

3

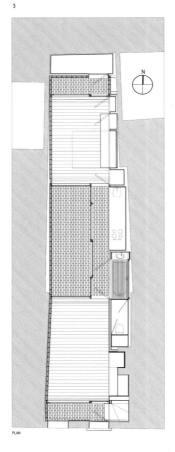

PLAN

This involved the remodelling of a single-storey terraced city cottage with a long site plot. The existing cottage was demolished, retaining the front façade and roof. The existing house plot is divided up by brick-lined courts, providing daylight and ventilation, and through the reflections in the glass, fill the interior with exterior views, and visa versa. A storage wall, lined in mahogany, is used to regulate the undulating geometry of the party wall, and contains a wall bed, wardrobes, doors, galley kitchen, bathroom, fireplace and stairs. The dormer room extension is glass-roofed and open to the brick-lined entrance court. Mahogany ope linings, windows and door complete openings in the front façade.

Area – 85m^2.
Stage – completed Spring 2003.

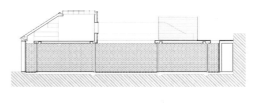

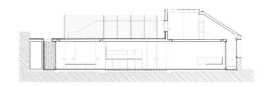

ASSESSORS' COMMENTS

CONROY – The position of the stairs in the plan challenges the nature, or expected nature, of this long, narrow house.

O'NEILL – I like the plan. It's a much stronger scheme than it might have been, and it has made something of itself.

BETSKY – This is a sophisticated project; it is spatially sophisticated. This project has a very tight space and it does something with it. The little slot for the shower I think is quite cute. The only thing I couldn't understand is they talk about a mahogany wall that accommodates everything, but I can only see a brick wall and a stucco wall. I thought that this was going to be all mahogany, but it's just stucco.

ROBBRECHT – I think that this is strong. It's a tiny space with all these follow-ups, which is like a series of images that are projected one on the other. It's an interesting approach. There's this enfilade of spaces which I like also.

BETSKY – This is an enfilade of spaces that gains a fair amount of continuity from a very tight environment, and manages to organise the ancillary spaces in a rather elegant form. I don't think it's a particularly great space. Again, as soon as you put one piece of furniture in here you lose a lot of the effect, but I think it's the most sophisticated project here of this type.

CONROY – I think it's very clever. It's thoughtful about that exact dimension of the space they've cut out, and the control of the wall. It's very elegant.

FINUCANE – I like the way the space flows through it, and the way you can see right through it. I think it's a much more sophisticated solution than the other conversion extensions we have seen.

CONROY – The thing that worries me a little bit about this one – and it's an issue that arises every year in the AAI Awards – is a slightness of achievement. Wrestling a school to the ground is a really big job, and then this thing isn't, and yet they're up there proudly sitting beside one another. I know you can't be comparing apples with oranges, but there does come a moment...

ARCHITECTS BATES MAHER – practice established in 2002 by Kevin Bates and Tom Maher.
KEVIN BATES – born in Clonmel, 1972. Studied architecture at University College Dublin, graduating in 1996.

TOM MAHER – born in Kilkenny, 1969. Studied architectural technology at Waterford Institute of Technology, graduating in 1989; studied architecture at UCD, graduating in 1995.

ARCHITECTS BATES MAHER
22 Lower Rathmines Road, Dublin 6
T 01-4914531 / 4914551 / F 01-4914531
E office@architectsbm.com
W www.architectsbm.com

3, 4, 5 TEMPLE COTTAGES, Dublin 7

BOYD CODY ARCHITECTS

This project presented us with a unique opportunity to convert three small terraced artisan houses into one dwelling. In the design, we wished to retain the integrity of the three existing houses. Each house is extended, and the addition is configured to maximise the natural light at the rear. A spatial matrix is thus created, both internally and externally, that relates closely to the workings of the house as whole.

House 3 accommodates on both floors the bathrooms, utility room and the vertical circulation, and in the addition is a studio at ground floor and a west-facing external terrace at first floor. House 4 internally holds the living area. It opens across houses 4 and 5 to form a room of generous proportion, and on to a courtyard at the rear. The original front doors are retained as shutters to glazed doors behind. A third bedroom and landing are located at first floor. House 5 has the dining area and a second bedroom at first floor, held within the existing footprint. In its addition are the kitchen and master bedroom. The master bedroom is located here in order to catch the morning light.

A strong spatial dialogue is created across the rear courtyard between the kitchen and the studio at ground-floor level. This is further reinforced by a concrete bench that moves across the back wall to form a work top in the kitchen, the steps to the courtyard, and a desk in the studio. The rear wall of the existing houses is expressed singularly through the use of a continuous rendered surface. These spaces all work, together with the living area, to provide free movement in this area through full-height sliding doors and screens.

This dialogue continues at first floor between master bedroom and terrace. The area is surrounded by a large translucent glazed screen. The screen provides privacy from the flats located behind the house. It also acts as a large reflector during the day, bringing light down into the courtyard, and as an illuminator at night, as it is artificially lit from behind.

The palette of materials is distilled down to glass, steel, iroko and plaster. The only introduction of colour is the orange of the kitchen and the shelves of the studio, which act as a counterpoint. A large illuminated installation piece was designed with the client (an artist) for the first-floor landing in order to provide image and light to this passageway.

Area – 160.7m². Stage – completed December 2002.

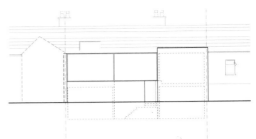

Section through bedroom and courtyard

Rear elevation

Original ground and 1st floor plans

New ground and 1st floor plans

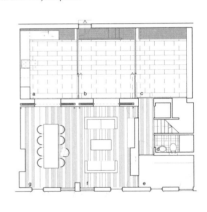

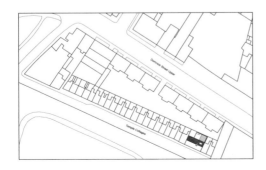

ASSESSORS' COMMENTS

BETSKY – They took three houses and made them into one. It's a bit like that Beatles movie, *Help*.

FINUCANE – I also thought that this project would have that surprise element, like in *Help*, when you walk in the door.

ROBBRECHT – What I think is very well solved is the six spaces. If you look at the plan, you have three houses, and then six spaces, and they all have their own identities. And then it comes to this – there's a courtyard, there's a balcony. But I think it's very well resolved, and there are some qualities in it.

CONROY – I was wondering would they keep the three front doors. The circularity of the plan gets past the predictability of linear circulation.

ROBBRECHT – Although it's a very rigid way of composing, there are some pleasant aspects.

BETSKY – But then there are some fingernail-on-the-blackboard things, to me. Like that wall there – that fake archaeological wall – and this interior here, with, yet again, those heavy wood-framed windows.

ROBBRECHT – Yes, that's true. But when I look at the cross-section, I have immediate interest in it.

FINUCANE – I think they have come up with a solution I could live with very, very easily. I take your point that that's a bit daft in places, but accidents happen in all lives. But I think the way the light goes down through the centre courtyard, and that you can look down into it from above is lovely. It's a nice house.

CONROY – I think that little yard has a Tadao Ando quality, and the control of light and views is of a high order.

DERMOT BOYD – born in 1967. Graduated from Dublin Institute of Technology in 1990, after completing a moderatorship in History of Art at TCD in 1998. Worked with Alberto Campo Baeza in Madrid and John Pawson in London. Returned to Ireland in 1992, and worked in private practice and with McCullough Mulvin. Currently teaches at DIT. PETER CODY – born 1967. Graduated from DIT, 1990. Masters at Columbia University (1995-96), research project in 1997. Worked with Alvaro Siza Viera in Porto (1992-95). Subsequently worked in New York, and returned to Ireland to commence private practice in 1998. Taught at DIT (1998-2000), and currently teaches studio at UCD. Formed Boyd Cody Architects in 2000.

DESIGN TEAM – Dermot Boyd, Peter Cody, Jim Corbett, Ryan Kennihan

BOYD CODY ARCHITECTS
The Studio, 15 Upper Baggot Street, Dublin 4
T 01-6677277 / F 01-6677278
E info@boydcodyarch.com
W www.boydcodyarch.com

ON HOUSING 3

Roland Bosbach, BSPL

Reality Check – Ideas and a somewhat naive creativity are the most valuable assets to young architects, assets which allow them to explore scenarios beyond the restrictions of the market and the confines of professional realism, scenarios that can provoke, gloss over the unsolvable, or simply rewrite reality to open up new ways of thinking. But in order to make a living and to receive proper recognition in a conservative profession, they have to mature, and prove themselves and their ideas in the 'real' world. The three domestic projects presented document the start of this maturation, and reflect the transformation of theoretical investigations into an application to the reality of the construction process, with real clients, neighbours, planners, conservation officers and building contractors.

Integration of Landscape – One main area of theoretical investigation has been the integration of landscape into the architecture of sub/urban forms to enhance the atmospheric and spatial diversity of their context, and to multiply territory, to create an informal background to continuously changing domestic schedules in which the programmatic terminology of each room becomes relative, and rooms are more characterised by adjacency and materiality than by programme. These three projects, all domestic extensions to existing houses, attempt to apply this investigation to their specific context with different strategies.

In HO1 a new extension establishes a kitchen, large enough to cook, work and rest in, on the first floor. It functions as a new hub between the main house and the back garden. Its built form sets up four urban landscape elements – front garden, sunken patio, breakfast terrace and back garden – allowing each room in the house establish a unique landscape-related quality in addition to their functional and spatial definition.

The extension in HO6 makes use of the existing two-level garden. By stepping up to the raised level, the roof opens up to provide a visual link back to the new informal roof ter-

Views of HO1 left and HO6 right, with HO8 opposite

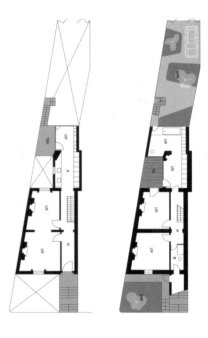

race and the old house, while allowing south sunlight to penetrate the new living spaces.

In HO8, a three-storey Victorian terrace – a protected structure with a north-facing garden – receives a new interface between garden and house. The roof of the extension splits and folds to allow maximum penetration of light while forming a visual extension and addition to the back garden.

Losing Control – The three projects also reflect an investigation into the process of anonymous detailing, a design process where the focus is on the conceptual coding of a typology rather than its formal expression in architectural details, on the development of designs that can be reproduced in a variety of styles and materials. Due to budget constraints, all three projects were carried out using direct labour.

HO1 – Area – 150m^2 (extension 21m^2). Stage – completed December 2002.
HO6 – Area – 105m^2 (extension 25m^2). Stage – completed June 2003.
HO8 – Area – 210m^2 (extension 36m^2). Stage – completed November 2003.

pages 130-131 – On Housing 3 – HO1

On Housing 3 – HO6

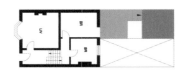

On Housing 3 – HO8

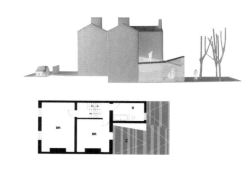

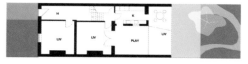

ASSESSORS' COMMENTS

CONROY – The spaces are cool, aren't they?

BETSKY – One space |HO6 – garden room with sloping roof|. I'm not sure I like that.

O'NEILL – I like those two more cubic extensions, HO1 and HO8.

ROBBRECHT – It's a mystery how this one |HO6, with the sloping roof| works. It looks very dramatic.

BETSKY – Slice the presentation panels down the middle, and only show the bottom two projects |HO1 and HO8|.

CONROY – I like them as projects. It's just I don't get the larger theme. And I'm not sure if the project is strengthened or weakened by the description: 'Ideas and a somewhat naive creativity are the most valuable assets to young architects', etc, etc.

BETSKY – Oh, weakened.

ROBBRECHT – All the photos are black and white, and I think this is hiding things that are not really very beautiful in reality. But, you know, how you detail these things is important. There are some Brutal qualities in it. You have such a small space here, and then you have this enormous thing. Several things which I don't particularly like are sometimes interesting. I don't know. There are very different aspects to the thing, and that's what I like. It's very different.

FINUCANE – I have to say I think that two-storey one looks rather nice |HO1|, and I like that one over there |HO8|.

ROBBRECHT – Presences. I like this one, which you mentioned also. There's another presence, and all in this project, that I appreciate. But, on the other hand, I am very doubtful about how it looks in reality. And how is the quality of the interior spaces?

O'NEILL – I like the substance of all this rhetoric. It doesn't take itself too seriously, and I think that's a good thing. They are quite simple in reality, I think.

CONROY – What I like is that there are three projects within a very specific and reductive vocabulary, and yet they each have quite distinct spatial qualities. That one with the children |HO8| is quite a bravura space.

BETSKY – Guys, we're looking here at overblown bourgeois minimalism, and we're trying to turn it into something grand.

ROLAND BOSBACH – born in Germany in 1970. Graduated from TU Dresden in 1999, and set up BSPL in Dublin.

BSPL
27a North Great Georges Street, Dublin 1
T 087-6487692 / E bspl@eircom.net

LIMERICK COUNTY COUNCIL HQ,
Dooradoyle, Limerick

BUCHOLZ McEVOY ARCHITECTS

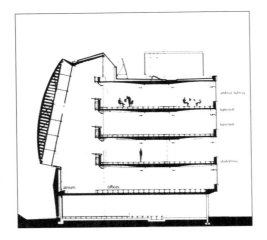

The project is for a new headquarters building for Limerick County Council, to accommodate and enhance the public services offered by the council, and to provide office space for its 230 employees.

Site Design Strategy – There is a strong link between the semi-natural open space along the Ballynaclough River and the headquarters site. The site is a gateway to this ecosystem. It is located at a 'hinge' between the semi-natural open space which follows the Ballinacurragh creek, and a large shopping centre surrounded by parking. The new headquarters creates a green edge along the Dooradoyle Road.

The large timber screen brise-soleil on the west elevation is inclined at 5° towards the sky, catching its reflections, and the ground plane is inclined up at 15°, creating a hinge between sky and ground.

As a building of civic importance, the new headquarters should be visible from both the N20 and the M20, clearly establishing itself as civic architecture legible at speed.

Environmental Strategy: Tuned In – The headquarters is an entirely naturally ventilated building. Mechanical ventilation has been designed out by 'tuning in' the building's fabric, structure and skin to the environment. The building's orientation, 15° rotated from north to south, allows the atrium to be the engine of the ventilation of the building, acting as a long thermal chimney. The offices are ventilated through cross-ventilation with the maximum office width 12.7m. The east elevation introduces air through BMS-controlled windows at high level, and the west façade controls the sun, allowing the atrium to heat up enough to induce ventilation across the offices. The aim is to passively control the building's temperature.

Area – 7,100m². Stage – completed October 2003.

■ *Editors' Note – In spite of repeated requests over a four-month period, the architects did not supply any drawings, photographs or biographical information for publication.*

ASSESSORS' COMMENTS

CONROY – There's a whole spate of these new public buildings in Ireland which are intended as a reassertion of local democracy. Some of them are fantastic buildings on very poor sites, and some of them are very poor buildings on fantastic sites. This is an unfortunate site – it's in the middle of an industrial estate in Dooradoyle. It's a very poor setting, and it's an attempt to make both figure and ground. It's both the datum and the object, which I think makes it difficult to do. It's immaculately built, and an incredible leap forward in construction technology. The council chamber is a beautiful room.

O'NEILL – And things were considered very specifically for it, and made very specifically for it, like the floor and the timber brise-soleil.

BETSKY – What really struck me, is how almost all these projects are completely divorced from their context.

CONROY – I think that's a very fair comment.

FINUCANE – I presume the setting is quite a bleak place and it is trying to do something for the place. Maybe it's a statement about local democracy and trying to brighten and cheer up the place. But I have to say, my initial reaction would be that I think it's enormously fussy. Maybe the presentation is not a true representation of how it looks in reality, because it does look awfully busy.

O'NEILL – The façade is much calmer in reality. They've made it look very busy in the presentation. It is, in fact, very beautiful.

CONROY – The big timber bows and the length of the façade have a certain grandeur. It has a civic nature that's unusual, without resorting to colonnades or to an older language. Its language is also somehow coded into energy and renewable sources, which gives it a kind of moral purpose. That's what I like about it.

FINUCANE – As you are describing it, it sounds like something much more gentle in the suburban landscape.

BETSKY – I really don't understand the plan, and we are not given the information that allows me to understand the plan. And so, what's going on?

O'NEILL – Well, that's the accommodation the brief has. It has the civic reading, and it has offices, and the offices have to behave environmentally. I think that's what that drawing is trying to say.

BETSKY – Why does it take the council chamber and all the things that should be the public spaces, and put them in that ugly orange box, completely outside of that big gesture? Inside it looks beautiful, but the box on the outside looks horrible. I mean that's your council chamber, that big orange pillbox?

O'NEILL – What they haven't done is shown the site, because I think those decisions were informed by its location. It is a very demanding site.

ROBBRECHT – I'm not convinced at all by this type of project. It doesn't impress me. So much gesture. The only thing is looking at the floors of the building and the shape, maybe that's interesting. And there's the thought of energy-efficiency.

FINUCANE – This project has seriously thought of energy-efficiency. I have to say I like that aspect. But I don't like that back elevation.

CONROY – The back elevation is grim.

O'NEILL – I must say, I like the section.

FINUCANE – Yes, so do I.

CONROY – All the public are on this floor and the decks open up. It's an old cliché, the openness suggesting democracy, and that, but it has a meaning there.

ROBBRECHT – But look at the section. I mean, look at the proportions! And if you need to do this angular thing [at top] with a curved façade like that, it's very strange.

BETSKY – I'm not so happy about it either. I'm very torn, because I think the screen could be beautiful, but then it looks like it's been made much too complex. You say, Antoinette, it's much quieter in reality, but in these photographs it looks too busy.

CONROY – There are energy concerns about the making of the façade as well, softened with timber.

BETSKY – Yes, but if you hadn't made it all glass, it wouldn't have to do all that stuff. I mean, those cubicles do not look very happy living underneath that space, however nice the light might be. It's a lot of ado, and I wonder, in the end, is it that terrific? We are never shown the ground floor. As far as I can tell, you enter somewhere here.

CONROY – You come up onto the deck.

BETSKY – Well, as far as I can tell from here, you enter here in front of the orange pillbox. Either that, or you're entering here on an upper level. Either way, you're entering in the system, sort of in the middle, and it doesn't seem to go anywhere at either end. And there's no acknowledgement in the plan of the relationship between civic spaces and this, what is essentially a kind of corridor for the bureaucrats over there.

CONROY – The public desks are all along that, that's what that is. That's a large public hall with licences and planning and housing, and all that sort of thing.

BETSKY – And what does that space look like? What does it look like underneath there?

CONROY – You can see the sense of it here with all the seats. I do think there's a certain aspiration in finding a civic language that's not dependent on older models, and that somehow has light and space and access coded into it.

BETSKY – But what does it say? I mean, this says a traditional thing, that you know, this is a somewhat monumental place of the people's power, but what does this part say: 'Bureaucrats are people too'?

CONROY – Think of the public arena, a well-lit hall where the public do their business, and there's a determination that they – not the bureaucrats – enjoy the volume.

O'NEILL – I think it's really interesting what you are saying about context, and the fact that they pointed out this. I think again – and I don't want to take it down to the local thing too much – but what people traditionally saw as their one-stop-shop where they went to get their licences and stuff was so grim.

FINUCANE – Grim and grotty, dreary and dark.

O'NEILL – Yes. I think that's part of that thing: look we'll offer you this now, this public building, it's your building.

CONROY – The weakest aspects of it are the civic elements, and in a way they don't activate the bar of offices. If you think about buildings where the fluctuation of the circulation is what drives the specific elements of the programme... That's what missing in this.

O'NEILL – The presentation could be a result of the architects having been in the Venice Biennale, which was all about building, the actual building, and pieces of building. And they brought mock-ups of that floor, and they brought the strut they had at the top, and they brought one of those beams, and they arranged them in a pavilion in Venice. It was a very convincing presentation of the project. So they were really investigating the building itself, and the context was not paramount. This presentation doesn't compare to Venice, understandably.

FINUCANE – Well I think, listening to you, that clearly what we are looking at is not what you have seen as a building.

O'NEILL – No. I think it's really a contender for the medal.

CONROY – It's heartbreaking if it is. But they didn't put the effort into showing it to best advantage, and that's what happens.

O'NEILL – It's a very important building.

CONROY – I think it is. I think if you saw it in reality, you'd be convinced there's a real civic grandeur in it.

BUCHOLZ McEVOY ARCHITECTS
Unit C Mountpleasant Industrial Estate, Upper Mount Pleasant Avenue, Rathmines, Dublin 6
T 01-4966340 / F 01-4966341 / E mbucholz@indigo.ie

PERISCOPE, Pembroke Lane, Dublin 4

GERARD CARTY ARCHITECT

The site is located on a mews lane to the rear of large 19th-century houses fronting onto Pembroke Road. Formerly the site of a coach house, it lay derelict for some years. It was considered important that the existing stone-walled boundaries, and the mature and semi-mature trees occupying the interstitial space between the mews and the main houses be retained as far as possible. The programme was to provide two houses which matched the different requirements of the owners – one, a family with small children, and the other a couple who entertain regularly at home.

The site was divided into two equal plots, 5.5m wide x 31m long, with a southerly aspect to the lane. Both houses have been developed with the main living spaces on the ground floor relating to a front courtyard and rear garden, and the bedroom and other accommodation on the upper level relating to a south-facing terrace. While differences exist between the houses in terms of internal layout, the intention was to develop a homogeneous external expression which would allow the resulting building to occupy the site coherently at the scale of the larger context. The ground floor of each house, captured between parallel walls, is largely open-plan in order to enjoy the full dimension of the site. Entrance areas, stores and cloakrooms are housed in a timber pavilion which projects forward into the front courtyard. This allows the remainder of the ground floor to exist as a largely uninterrupted space, save for sliding and fixed screens which allow kitchen areas to be closed-off if required. It is at first-floor level where the greater differences between the houses is evident. Where one house contains three bedrooms, bathroom and a reading room (part of a flexible and convertible landing space), the other contains one bedroom, bathrooms, dressing room, and a large flexible room which acts as library and guest room.

Structurally the houses are developed using a cross-wall method tied with wall beams to the front and rear. The front wall beam contains a south-facing terrace at first floor, providing a privacy screen. To the rear, the beam spanning across both houses provides a cill to fix a timber and glass screen which relates to the immediate environment of trees and gardens, and provides a single scale when viewed from the main house.

The term 'periscope' pertains to the manner in which the houses strive to reach beyond the restrictions imposed by the conflicting demands of light, views, privacy and scale by means of the section.

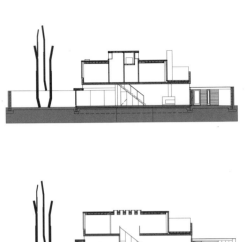
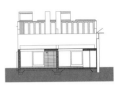
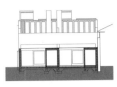

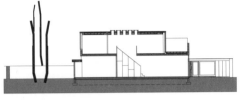

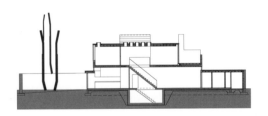

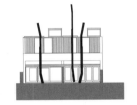

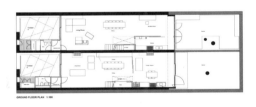

GROUND FLOOR PLAN 1:100

FIRST FLOOR PLAN 1:100

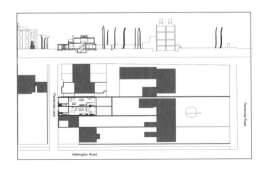

143

ASSESSORS' COMMENTS

CONROY – I didn't really get the periscope thing.

BETSKY – Yes, I sort of was intrigued by that.

CONROY – They're clever plans, simple and adaptable, and it's all quite well made – bright, convincing rooms.

O'NEILL – This is an interesting example of domestic work.

BETSKY – There are some nice things here and there.

CONROY – That's quite nice, I thought, with the leg and the light.

FINUCANE – I like this project. It mightn't be enormously remarkable being a pair of mews houses, but I like it very much.

BETSKY – It's very pleasant. One of the things I liked from the outset was the way it inter-locks the two houses in the one façade, so that each has an identity, and yet it's a communal building as an object. And the inside has some very delicate moments, very nice compositions of windows. But then, on the other hand, it's a generic space with spotlights hanging from the ceilings, and there's a lack of definition. When you look at that poor little couch, in front of that half-wall, it feels lost. It's as if they con-trolled all the edges, both on the inside and the outside, and as soon as it goes to the middle, and you have to actually make some rooms, there doesn't seem to be much there.

FINUCANE – That's when the clients take over. What's happening there over that balcony? Is that opening and closing back?

BETSKY – Yes, there's a big pivoting wall making the reading room.

O'NEILL – I think what's interesting about these houses is they are furnished too, so we are seeing how people actually live in it. I mean, I take what you are saying about the sofa, but at least we are seeing it. It feels as if you could live here. And I think the quality of light throughout it is nice.

BETSKY – We are seeing what it is. That's very true. I think that should be in the jury com-ments, as encouragement for next year, to furnish the interiors of buildings. You can't fool us!

ROBBRECHT – It's an okay double-house. Nice corners. These sections I liked also. The edges are the strongest part, true.

GERARD CARTY – graduated from DIT School of Architecture, 1987. Worked with Tod Wakefield in London, McGarry NíÉanaigh Architects, and Vazquez Consuegra in Seville. Winner of AAI Awards in 1989 and 1998. Associate director at Grafton Architects.

DESIGN TEAM – Gerard Carty, Eva Byrne, Michael Wall, Simon Nugent

GERARD CARTY
73 Pembroke Road, Dublin 4 – T 01-6689411

ALLINETT'S LANE APARTMENTS, Cork

MV CULLINAN ARCHITECTS

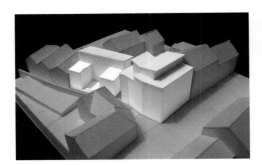 

This is an urban infill project which sets out to demonstrate that apartment living can support higher-density development without undue loss of privacy or amenity. The steeply sloping site, located on the corner of Gerald Griffin Street and Allinett's Lane, has views out over the city. Allinett's Lane connects Gerald Griffin Street to Watercourse Road – both significant routes into the city centre. Blackpool, on the north side of Cork, has numerous historic lanes, but recent developments have relegated many of them to service access only.

In this scheme, two buildings of five and seven apartments are organised around a small paved square and a shared courtyard. The buildings step down from the street to the lane, and this stepping in section is mirrored in plan, where the façade is faceted along the outer edges. This combination of stepping and faceting allows the buildings turn the corner and reduce in scale in response to the existing streetscape.

The smaller building is located on the lane, and laid out to support its use as an inhabited thoroughfare. The building steps back to allow light into the lane, and opens to form a small paved square around which are five apartments. There are no internal common areas. The door of each apartment opens, via a private threshold, onto a circulation

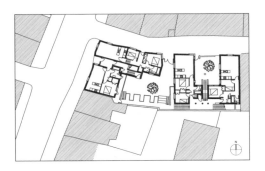

route, which passes up and through the building. All apartments have access to the shared facilities via this route, through and around the buildings. Here, in the shared courtyard, a terrace with drying 'piers' for laundry extends over screened bicycle and bin stalls. These, together with small children's theatre steps, provide a safe play area easily monitored from the apartments.

All units have dual-aspect rooms opening onto balconies or terraces which face either south or west. The buildings are painted plaster with treated softwood windows and aluminium cills and copings.

Site – 476m²

Area – 730m² (comprising eleven 55m² 2-bed apartments and one 40m² 1-bed apartment)

Density – 102 units per acre (252 units/ha); 289 bedspaces per acre (714 bedspaces/ha)

Stage – completed Sept 2003

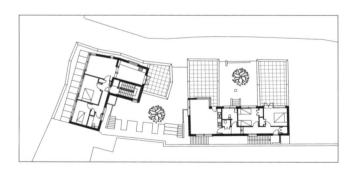

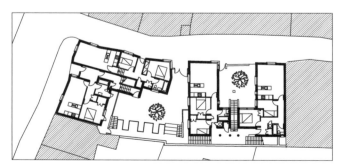

ASSESSOR'S COMMENTS

CONROY – I'm kind of fascinated by this project. But then I look at the courtyard photo, and if there are two words that make your heart sink, it's 'birdbath sculpture'.

FINUCANE – Oh, you're very cynical. I like the way it fits in between the other buildings.

BETSKY – The planning is very nice.

CONROY – I think what is interesting about this project is it activates a backland site, and it contains a goodly amount of accommodation. What I don't like about it is the wall-paper nature of the rendered elevation. It's poorly made is what's disappointing.

O'NEILL – The elevations are quite banal. It's when it comes to the elevational detail that it goes wrong. It's like somebody did the planning, and somebody else the detailing. It's like two different buildings. When I look at the plan, it's very well done.

CONROY – It's careful about amenity. If you look at the roof terraces, the living rooms, they're good quality. I think this is all quite well worked-out; the loggia and the laneway – it's just the right width.

ROBBRECHT – The elevations are not very well detailed. But I think it controverts to the urban situation. It's one of the projects that really shows where it is. It makes a kind of little street here, which probably works quite well. The elevations are poorly made, but there was very little money. It is local authority housing after all.

BETSKY – Really? It is? Oh, well, that's a plus for it then. I thought it was more deluxe than that. You have the bedrooms always in the quiet place, and the living rooms are always on the street, and you create these very nice courtyards that you enter from the side. But maybe this [elevation] is a little bit strange.

FINUCANE – I just really like the way it fits into its context. I think it really works in its context with these hilly streets and lanes.

ROBBRECHT – Yes, that's true. I'm happy with this situation in this row of façades.

CONROY – What I also like about it, given particularly that it's local authority, there's very little to go wrong in terms of maintaining the place. It's kind of nailed down.

FINUCANE – Do you want to be quoted on that? That it has to be nailed down?

CONROY – Well, I do that type of work, so I don't mind saying it. I'm interested in it at that level. What I love about it is the scale and the increment, just the amount of distance between the buildings and the windows, and overlooking and self-regulation. All those things are very well worked out. I just think, like a lot of local authority work, the skin and the detailing is poor. But overall it's modest and sensible.

MV CULLINAN ARCHITECTS – established in 1997. Received an AAI Award in 1994 and RIAI Regional Awards in 1994, 1996, 1999 and 2000. In 1994, awarded the RIAI Triennial Silver Medal for Housing, 1991-1993. MICHAEL CULLINAN – studied at UCD and Harvard University. Studio lecturer at DIT (1991) and UCD (1991-2000). Elected a Fellow of the Royal Institute of Architects of Ireland in 2001.
DESIGN TEAM – Maxime Laroussi, Jitka Svobodova, Michael Cullinan, Bryan Johnston

MV CULLINAN ARCHITECTS
2 Essex Quay, Dublin 8 – T 01-6707566 / F 01-6707568 / E mvarch@indigo.ie

LIFFEY HOUSE, Tara Street, Dublin 2

DONNELLY TURPIN ARCHITECTS

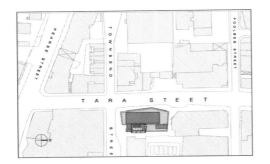

The building that previously stood on this prominent city-centre corner site was a poor-quality speculative office block built in the 1970s. It was six stories high and substantially set back parallel to the street line. The area in front of it was occupied by an unsightly surface car park.

In 1997, when Dublin City Council, who owned and occupied the building, acquired the strip of land in front of it, they commissioned a feasibility study as to how it might best be refurbished and extended to improve its function and appearance, and maximise the potential of the site. Massing studies and cost analysis indicated that full demolition and replacement with a substantially larger building was economically viable.

The City Council required a flexible, quality, commercial office block for rent on the open market. Their intention was twofold. They hoped to generate a stream of income to fund socially oriented projects across the city, and to set a standard of design and construction quality for private sector commercial developers. The bulk of the building, therefore, comprises undifferentiated floor plates in a shell state, awaiting one or more tenants.

As built, the building has six floors and a penthouse of office space over a ground-floor showroom and a basement-level car park and plant area. Service, landlord and ancillary areas are located at the rear of the site. The office accommodation faces west, with floor-to-ceiling glazing and views across the city. The main entrance is on the corner junction of Tara Street and Townsend Street. A separate entrance to the ground-floor showroom is provided on Tara Street.

The basic urban and architectural moves are simple. The rectangular ground-floor plan reinforces the orthogonal nature of the urban block. The ground-floor façade aligns with those of the adjoining office and apartment developments on both Tara Street and Townsend Street, and provides generous public pavement area. The bulk of the office accommodation is located overhead in a curvilinear form, which sails

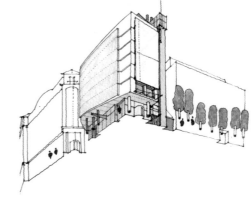

153

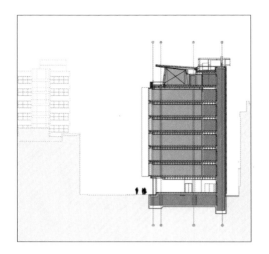

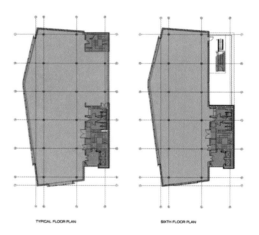

TYPICAL FLOOR PLAN   SIXTH FLOOR PLAN

close to the site boundary, projects to provide cover for the main entrance, and inflects to register the oblique entrance to the adjoining Ashford House. The intention was that the building would be both rooted in the context and appear to be dynamically moving.

Material choices, transparency, and apparent weight were the subject of much consideration. Each element is clearly expressed. Service and landlord accommodation is located in a slim rectangular block to the rear of the site and is clad in a common red brick, matching that of nearby traditional structures. The office accommodation is clad in a smooth curved wall of high-performance glass and black Chinese basalt. The stone is carried under to form the soffit and ground-floor ceiling. The mass of the building appears to float over the highly transparent ground floor.

Area – 5,500m².
Stage – completed December 2003.

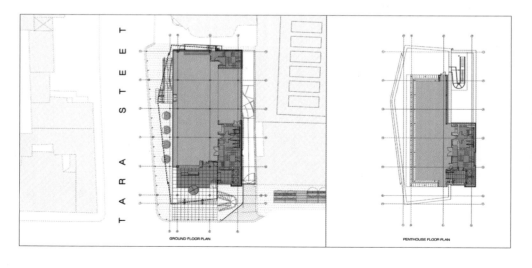

GROUND FLOOR PLAN   PENTHOUSE FLOOR PLAN

ASSESSORS' COMMENTS

O'NEILL – It's a beautiful building in its context. It's very sophisticated.

CONROY – It's a very nice building. It's so carefully made, and in its context, that bowed façade is really very elegant.

BETSKY – Why is that bow there?

CONROY – It's to do with the bend on the street. The 1960s office block previously on this site sat back from the street, and they replaced it with this one. And since they have, it's added a whole new dimension to the street.

O'NEILL – When you turn this corner, which is a huge corner from Pearse Street, it has a very strong presence.

CONROY – You can't see this aspect very well in the photographs. And it's also much more sophisticated. You begin to get a sense of line and planar control.

BETSKY – This lack of context illustrations is maddening. It looks like a really unpleasant relationship to the street at ground level.

O'NEILL – Where does it look like a really unpleasant relationship to the street? I can't agree with you.

CONROY – The skinny columns are a pity. The rest of this façade is so confident though. The cladding passes out and bends back in. It's all very well done, but that level of detail doesn't come up in the images.

FINUCANE – I didn't recognise it from the photographs at first, and yet I know I have come around that corner and thought, oh, I like that building.

ROBBRECHT – I must say, I like this bending façade, but what I'm wondering is if you have a short façade like that [on Townsend Street], why do you have so many elements in the elevation? What's the reason for this?

BETSKY – I don't like those big circular vents from the underground car park.

ROBBRECHT – It has some clichés like that, and yet if you look at the roof there, it's such a clever roof. Overall it has a really nice quality.

O'NEILL – It's very refined, yes.

CONROY – I think it's a very refined building. The cladding system is very elegant, and it's got these strong leading edges. It has a real presence on the street.

DONNELLY TURPIN ARCHITECTS – established by Charles Donnelly and Mark Turpin in 1997 – has completed a variety of projects both public and private, including the new parliamentary offices at Leinster House (in collaboration with the OPW) which was a recipient of both RIAI and Europa Nostra awards.

DESIGN TEAM – Charles Donnelly , Mark Turpin, and Achim Gottstein (project architect)

DONNELLY TURPIN ARCHITECTS
42 Dawson Street, Dublin 2
T 01-6711691/ F 01-6711692 / E dta@donnellyturpin.com

SPORTS AND YOUTH SERVICES CENTRE, Cabra, Dublin 7

HENCHION-REUTER ARCHITECTS

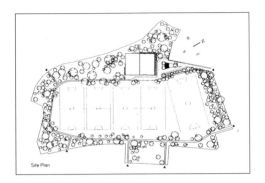

Site Plan

Pope John Paul II Park was developed from a disused railway shunting yard in the 1950s, and it is now an intensively used sports park with five football pitches and a running track. The brief was to develop these sports facilities and to provide accommodation for various community facilities. In particular, the local 'youth at risk' are to be targeted, and the building will be the base for seven youth services workers in the area.

On the ground floor the building provides six paired external changing rooms for the outdoor playing pitches. Each is an independently accessed self-contained unit with its own WC and showers. These facilities can be used without opening up the whole facility. Also accessed externally are the referees' changing room, changing rooms for the all-weather pitch, and three storerooms for nets and other equipment.

The main entrance faces the playing pitches, and the entrance 'forecourt' is an extension to the path circuiting the park. The main hall is a standard single sports hall, suitable for basketball, indoor soccer, badminton and volley ball. Other accommodation on the ground floor includes a dance studio, martial arts studio, and the main changing rooms. The main stairs leads directly to a canteen area at the first floor, which overlooks the main hall and the all-weather pitch. The fitness studios overlook the external playing pitches, and these can be subdivided with folding screens. A self-contained suite of rooms provides a childcare facility, with access to the timber decked terrace to the south-west. A number of other community rooms share access to this deck, which acts as a viewing gallery to the all-weather pitch below.

Various forms of rooflighting maximise lighting from above, and the section has been developed to capitalise on borrowed light where the plan is deepest. While the main studio spaces are calm and simple, the circulation spaces have been invested with incident and detail. Views through to neighbouring rooms and across the section of the building have been orchestrated to allow the participants to see and be seen. Colour has been introduced to respond to the moments of greatest light intensity. The project will be completed with the planting of 150 additional trees.

Area – 2,000m². Stage – completed December 2003.

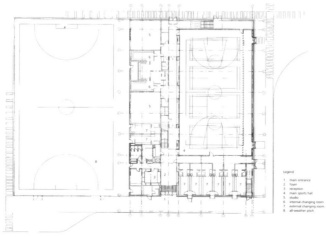

Legend

1. main entrance
2. foyer
3. reception
4. main sports hall
5. studio
6. internal changing room
7. external changing room
8. all-weather pitch

ASSESSORS' COMMENTS

CONROY – Yes, I like this. I think it's very confident.

BETSKY – You do? Tell me why.

CONROY – I think it's a low-budget project with a refined end-product.

BETSKY – With that kind of wood? That's not low-budget.

CONROY – I think it's a building that's going to be under pressure from the off, and yet it manages to set a tone about quality. And I like the use of the rooflights on the two sides, and the care about the walls and the stairs. I think it's in a difficult genre, and it's very carefully done.

BETSKY – This is a tough neighbourhood. But the security aspects are pretty nasty. Look at the use of colour. And look at that kind of detailing. I know, yes, it's cheap, but do you really have to use this kind of colours?

O'NEILL – I take what you're saying. I don't mind the colours, but I do think those doors are very chunky, and some of the photographs are hiding behind that black-and-white atmospheric photography. But there are many elements that are very well considered. And that gallery there works well overlooking the main space. Those kind of things are very considered, where it needs to be.

CONROY – I still think there's a clarity and a strength in it. And even this kind of technical ceiling, it's all quite simple. I think it has a rigour, and a clarity about movement and light and space that's very simple.

ROBBRECHT – I like the main elevation and the gallery overlooking the whole space. Something with the dimensions also tries to achieve some lightness. And even these fences here are considered.

O'NEILL – I think the plan is very rigorous, and I really like that image of the exterior at night. It's convincing as a programme.

FINUCANE – I like the timber structure and I find these photos very convincing.

BETSKY – If you had told me it was a youth prison I would have believed you. I think it goes over the fine line between being cheap and rugged and looking like it's cheap and rugged, and making you aware that you are only worth something that is cheap and rugged. Certain aspects of the design have escaped from that, like the use of light, and this strong wood image, but otherwise...

ROBBRECHT – It is not completely successful, I agree. But it does achieve something special with a limited budget in a difficult context.

MARTIN HENCHION – born in Cork, 1967 – and KLAUS REUTER – born in Bonn, 1964 – have been in practice in Germany since 1994, and in Dublin since 1998.
JULIA LOUGHNANE (project architect) – born in Dublin, 1977. Graduated from UCD in 2001.

HENCHION-REUTER ARCHITECTS
8 Parkview Place, Ringsend, Dublin 4
T 01-6674740 / F 01-6674741 / E info@henchion-reuter.com / W www.henchion-reuter.com

OFFICE FOR A COFFEE IMPORTER, Belfast

ALAN JONES ARCHITECTS

This project is a temporary office and showroom, set in a corner of a warehouse located within Belfast's busy harbour area. The area is overtly commercial, with speed of turn-around and low profit margins reflected by expedient buildings and neglected spaces.

We created an inwardly focussed interior, with incoming light and outward views through obscuring polycarbonate. The double skin on the gable wall and roof shimmer with natural and artificial light, obscuring the view of the warehouse, yet animating the office working environment.

The project was designed and constructed at short notice within a short programme to an extremely tight budget. Readily available ordinary materials – the type found in local DIY stores – form the basis of the palette of materials: medium density fibreboard, poly-carbonate, concrete blocks, plaster, carpet tiles and mill-finish aluminium. Plain steel-framed desks and a stair were fabricated off-site.

Location – Dargan Road, Belfast. Area – 50m². Stage – completed 2003.

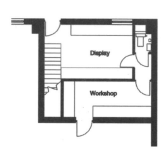

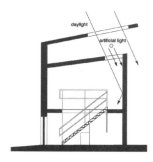

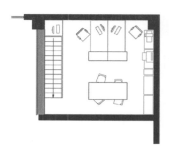

ASSESSORS' COMMENTS

CONROY – That panoramic view showing the office unit in its coffee warehouse context is a fantastic photo.

O'NEILL – It's a cheeky entry.

ROBBRECHT – I was interested in this. It's probably done with no money at all. I mean, it's a kind of avant-garde stuff. It's in a big warehouse with no windows, and it sucks the light from above. It's probably the project of a very young architect, a first work, and I would like to support it. I like the materials.

CONROY – I like the sensitivity of Paul's response to this small project.

ROBBRECHT – There's this strange thing, the relationship between the upper-floor office and what's going on around it; it seems to be really quiet. And it even has toilets and things.

FINUCANE – I'm sort of taken aback in some ways that this project is even being considered. But now that I have heard some of the arguments in favour of it, my heart has been moved. I like the notion of it being done on a shoestring, maybe by somebody who is just starting out.

CONROY – It's incredible – it's all sheet-plastic, is what it is.

ROBBRECHT – I think it was built in one afternoon!

BETSKY – We should put it in the exhibition as a good example of a young architect's work. It's a nice antidote to some of the overly worked minimalism we've seen. It's also a skilful photographer at work.

ALAN JONES – studied architecture at Queen's University Belfast. Practised in London with Michael Hopkins, and as an associate with David Morley. Returned to Ulster in 1998, where he teaches and practices architecture. The practice was published by the Architecture Foundation, London, as part of their *New Architects* series. Current projects include a community arts facility in Strabane, Co Tyrone.

ALAN JONES ARCHITECTS
37 Malone Road Belfast BT9 6RX – T 048-90667789 / F 048-90667567
E admin@jonesarchitects.com / W www.jonesarchitects.com

MORTUARY CHAPELS AND POSTMORTEM SUITE, St James's Hospital, Dublin

Derek G Byrne, HENRY J LYONS & PARTNERS

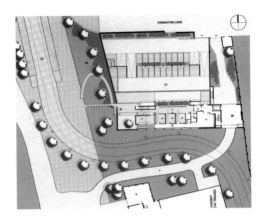

The Luas light rail system, connecting Dublin city centre with Tallaght town centre to the west of the city, will pass through St James's Hospital, providing a rail stop adjacent to the main public entrance off James's Street. The agreed route necessitated the demolition of a number of existing facilities and the construction of replacement facilities in alternative locations. These included new laundry, mortuary and postmortem suite facilities, and ancillary storage, plant and car-parking facilities. The mortuary and postmortem suite and stores are arranged in a single new building, with adjoining car park, to the west of the new light rail stop, with a landscaped park in-between.

The building takes the form of a 54m x 10m two-and-a-half-storey-high rectilinear block, set back, southwards, 33m from, and parallel to, a public road, Ewington Lane. The lower, semi-basement houses the stores. The mezzanine (ground) floor, 1.5m above the surrounding topography, provides the public chapels and body storage facilities, while the postmortem suite is located at first-floor level. The site between the building and Ewington Lane provides a semi-basement and mezzanine car park, the deck levels of which correspond to the stores and public chapels within. It is entered and exited via Ewington Lane. The car park and circulation pattern is designed to allow a cortege to form in the parking areas, and leave the facility in a dignified and orderly fashion.

The ensemble of building and car park is separated from the light rail stop to the west by a new landscaped park, an inclined plane of grass and trees through which pedestrians arriving by bus or light rail will enter the chapels.

The building and car park are wrapped at ground level to the south and west in continuous 3.3m high white, polished, precast-concrete walls, punctured only once by the mortuary pedestrian entrance in the park, creating a sort of enclave within the wider hospital campus. The postmortem suite 'floats' above the polished walls, and is clad in a flat, aluminium rain-screen skin, finished in the green hue of patinated copper. Large and small openings afford views from within, but these are screened with aluminium slats to maintain operational privacy and reduce heat-gain on the south and west façades. The structure throughout is cast-in-situ reinforced concrete.

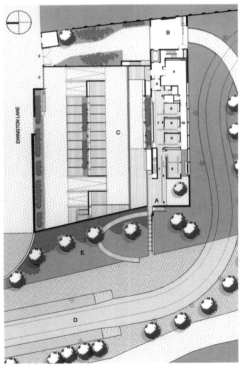

Ground floor plan

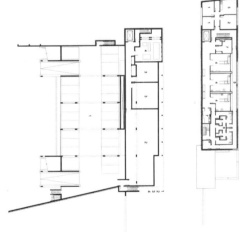

Basement plan   1st floor plan

North and south elevations
Cross-section and west elevation

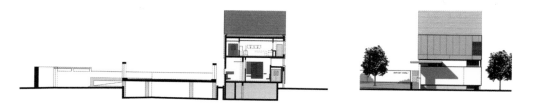

To meet the hospital's operational requirements, the building is layered in plan and section. The public entrance is via a quiet, enclosed, landscaped courtyard at the west gable, gathering visiting mourners arriving by car or public transport and guiding them into the 24m long reception hall. The long hall provides an access strip into the chapels, which form a second layer buried in the centre, the heart, of the plan. The third layer inside the southern façade is the private, discreet service corridor, which communicates between the body preparation area and the chapels. The postmortem suite on the top floor is similarly layered from north to south, consecutively, by the autopsy rooms access corridor, the rooms themselves, and the student viewing gallery, which also provides staff access into the changing suite.

While the public entrance is located at the western end of the building, the service and staff entrance is at the extreme opposite end, to the east. Discreet entry is provided off Ewington Lane for the delivery of deceased patients and supplies, separate from the carpark entry. A covered service compound is located under the building, large enough to

allow hearses to turn, and exits back onto Ewington Lane. Larger delivery trucks, along with ambulances, also enter via the Ewington Lane service route, but exit from the service compound, back onto the campus, across the light rail track. The stacked layers of stores, mortuary chapels and postmortem suite are connected vertically by a lift and stairs, both accessed from the covered service compound at ground level.

The postmortem suite has been designed to the highest medical standards, incorporating the latest planning techniques and equipment for morbid anatomy. The mortuary chapels provide the setting for the most traumatic and emotional first, and sometimes only, direct encounter for family and friends with their deceased loved one. The architectural approach and arrangement was deeply concerned with reconciling, in an appropriately reticent and dignified manner, the secular science of pathology with the religious ritual and spiritual process of death.

Area – 1,349m². Stage – completed Summer 2003 (excluding landscaping).

ASSESSORS' COMMENTS

BETSKY – At first glance, it's very sophisticated, very beautiful, very elegant. Of course, if you can't do that in a mortuary chapel, you're in trouble. But then I start to look specifically, and I wonder why does it have to be this very thin building with all the chapels lined up, so that there's a very thin waiting area. You also reduce yourself to these two thin boxes sliding over each other as the image of the chapel, in this green metal, and I don't quite understand that either.

O'NEILL – But that's just so beautiful, that photograph of the chapel.

BETSKY – Yes, there are some beautiful moments.

FINUCANE – You can nearly feel a spiritual quality at the way it is done. But from reading the plan, I think that it would be a source of such heartbreak to people to try and figure out in which one of those chapels is their dead relative. But other than that I think it's absolutely beautiful.

BETSKY – Do you understand this [south] elevation? What does it mean, what does it say?

ROBBRECHT – That was my first thought. I nearly couldn't believe this was a mortuary. I'm ever more away from this than the library [Tubbercurry]. It's not touching me at all.

FINUCANE – Do you not like those interior spaces?

ROBBRECHT – No. Possibly the way the light is treated there, this direct light. But this is not a spiritual place.

O'NEILL – Gosh! I really like this work. But for me a building doesn't have to look like a mortuary. We have so many places that try too hard to look religious. This just seemed like a really elegant solution. And the spirituality is important, which, for me, is really well achieved. That chapel space is just so beautiful. Maybe it's the consideration of how this was put together as well. Somebody has really considered it.

FINUCANE – Well, you know, even at a small funeral in Ireland you are going to have fifty people. It's just one of those things that has to be handled with enormous dignity, and not have people kind of going to the wrong coffin, which is horrendous.

CONROY – It's all very careful, including the covered public entrance where you can stand out of the rain. It's thoughtful.

BETSKY – Why is it this a rigid bar? Would it have had more room if it had been this slight angle, if it had gotten fatter at one point? And you can then use that compression to get, for instance, a way to move through to another area where there is more room for the chapels.

O'NEILL – You can say it's easy to make these nice moments, but we should commend this quality. This is an award for architectural excellence, and saying 'you did it well but that is not enough' is too easy somehow. It should be considered for an award.

DEREK BYRNE – born in 1959. Worked with VB Gallagher & Associates from 1975 to 1978. Studied at DIT Bolton Street from 1978 to 1981. Working with Henry J Lyons & Partners since 1981.
DESIGN TEAM – Derek Byrne, Susan Mealy, Enda Cavanagh

HENRY J LYONS & PARTNERS
47-48 Pearse Street, Dublin 2 – T 01-8883333 / F 01-8883322 / E hjl@hjlyons.com / W www.hjlyons.com

HOWTH HOUSE, Co Dublin

O'DONNELL + TUOMEY ARCHITECTS

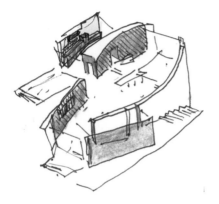

The clients had been living next door in a Victorian villa – a house of many rooms. They wanted a convivial living space which more loosely accommodated contemporary family life. The idea for the new house started from an introductory conversation held on the site. Looking out to sea, with the sun on our backs, we discussed with the client our shared preference for facing north, watching the effect of the light on the landscape without the glare of the sun in your eyes – the quiet of standing in the shadow and looking at the light. Halfway up the Hill of Howth, overlooking the harbour, the site lies sandwiched between houses, blinkered by its boundaries and mesmerised by the outline of the island of Ireland's Eye.

A three-part plan and sectional organisation grew out of the site conditions. The house was designed from the inside out, or from the sense of being within the site looking out, and each development in the form was designed from first principles. A long wall is aligned between two trees which fix diagonally opposite corners of the plot. The body of the house turns to focus on the island; the walls bend to cup the space that flows between them. The house is extended like a telescope. It is designed as a device for directing light through from the south and views out to the north, but its scale is determined by everyday domestic routines. Dimensions are set out from the fixed points of fireplace and kitchen, with the dining table as the centre of gravity around which the plan revolves.

The long walls are load-bearing; there are no columns or cross walls; the space flows on. Transparency is maintained along the length of the house, and the structure takes its lateral stability from concrete floor slabs. Concrete ceilings are boardmarked in correspondence with the floorboard pattern of the rooms. Timber floors turn up at their edges to make partitions and balustrades, avoiding any secondary detail of railings or skirtings. Spiralled inside their wooden boxes, the sky-lit shower rooms are tiled all over in glass mosaics. External brickwork is smeared over in grey-pigmented limewash, and internal wall surfaces are selectively painted to emphasise the effect of light and dark on the character of the house. Earth-based colours saturate one face of each longitudinal wall, with cross-cuts providing contrasting highlights in the linear structure.

Area – 280m². Stage – completed March 2003.

Long walls bend to cup the space

Lower-ground-floor plan

Ground-floor plan

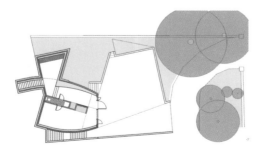

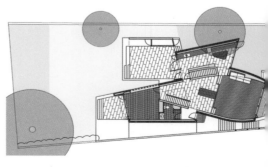

The house looks towards the island

1st floor plan   Longitudinal section

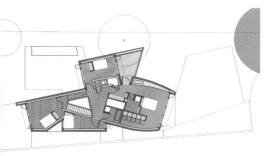 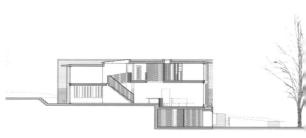

ASSESSORS' COMMENTS

O'NEILL – The walls show the way the architects were thinking about what's going on on this site. The walls cup the view, and follow the path of the sun.

FINUCANE – I have to say I really like it. I could live in it. The finish on the concrete, and the detailing of the timber, is so beautifully done, isn't it?

CONROY – It's a beautiful house. It's beautifully made as well.

BETSKY – I'm not sure I'm that convinced when you have to literally translate angles and points of view for geometric abstractions into physical form, and it gives you these kind of tortured shapes, and I wonder whether all of them are quite as wonderful as the photography makes them look. It also makes you create these massive parallel walls that kind of drown the house.

O'NEILL – I think that particular photograph might be exaggerating that effect in the middle of the house.

ROBBRECHT – It's well situated on its small site, although still very near other houses. But I would not live in a house with so little space in it. It's also a bit overactive in its geometry for my liking. But it's a nice house, I have to say.

O'NEILL – I take what you say about the geometry, but I think it is a really satisfying design. They are not wilful decisions; they are very much considered. And the materials and finishes throughout are beautiful.

ROBBRECHT – I particularly like the quality of light inside.

CONROY – The aesthetic of it inside is to do with these shapes pressing on each other, and the concrete and the timber. I think that's why that release through the hole in the slab is so powerful, because the rest of it is about compression, which I think gives it its character. The rooms are, when it gets down to it, pretty small. But I think it's a beautiful house.

BETSKY – We could have an endless debate about the geometry of the house. But I really don't buy the notion that you make a line, and say the view is there, and so that

means that you have to get that geometry as a physical wall. Why do the opposite walls of the living room have to do the same thing? But there are wonderful spaces in there as well. And the handling of materials is impressive.

CONROY – The combination of those spaces and materials – that's what's good about it. The detailing throughout is really compelling.

O'DONNELL + TUOMEY – founded in 1988 by Sheila O'Donnell and John Tuomey. The practice has developed an international reputation for cultural and educational buildings. (See p116 for full biography.)

O'DONNELL + TUOMEY ARCHITECTS
20a Camden Row, Dublin 8 – T 01-4752500
F 01-4751479 / E info@odonnell-tuomey.ie
W www.odonnell-tuomey.ie

AIRPORT BRIDGES
Northern Motorway / Airport-Balbriggan Bypass

ROUGHAN AND O'DONOVAN ENGINEERS with GRAFTON ARCHITECTS

Interchange at Dublin Airport (above and p191) – This project involved the design of a suite of bridges, two of which form the space of the roundabout, a space at the scale of the big landscape. There was, therefore, the potential to think of the outside and the inside of this space as being different. The form of the outside face of the bridge should be different to the inside face; the form and profile of the bridges would have to be strong enough to be clearly read at a distance and at high speed.

The structural solution was for a 60m long two-span in situ concrete bridge on a radius of 334m and a width of 15m. The leg of the central support pulls back into the round-about space, and the head leans out, nosing into the space of the motorway. The outer face is sharp, in an effort to cast shadows and contrast light and shade. The inner face is more mute, as the form will be viewed from a shorter distance. The deck sits asymmetrically on the column, cantilevers into the space of the motorway, and is at its minimum depth at the outer edge.

The soffit of the bridge offers a large surface to the outer face. The horizontal crease-line in the deck soffit pulls from the outer edge of the abutment to the central line of the column. The form gives a sense of tension and dynamic to the roundabout. The abutments stop short of the deck, both to house the movement joints, and to give the sense of continuity between the suspended deck and the road supported on formed groundworks.

Flyover Bridges on Airport-Balbriggan Bypass (opposite) – The single bridges were designed as a variation of the same approach. These offer the same elevations on both sides, and are more static. The profile is still angular for the same reasons of contrast of light and shade, and legibility of the form at a distance.

The engineers worked closely with the architects, and shared the ambition to give architectural expression to the structural workings of these bridges, and, in the case of the roundabout, to exploit the potential of making a momentary sense of containment and legibility within the spaceless world of the motorway traveller. This was done through the process of landscape models, detail study models and sketches, made in parallel with detailed technical structural drawings.

189

ASSESSORS' COMMENTS

O'NEILL – I like the way the strut is different on the inside and the outside. It's making a roundabout, and it's done that very deliberately. And I like the fact that there's an infrastructure project in contention in the Awards.

BETSKY – There's all this written about the roundabout, but the road pattern and rails all look fairly standard. The only thing the architect seems to have done was the bridge struts. But the struts are nice.

CONROY – It's somehow not enough though, is it? I keep looking at it and want to get really enthusiastic about it, but somehow it's still a roundabout. All the usual barriers, etc, are still there. It's beautifully done, but it somehow doesn't seem to have located the potential of the thing as a space.

O'NEILL – They could have done something more fundamental at design stage.

CONROY – It really drives me nuts when you drive down along and every bridge is slightly different, but they are all ultimately the same. And you know everybody has got top fees on each of them. I would imagine that they should all be completely different or exactly the same. In a way, this isn't that radically different from the bridges further up. I mean, it's better, but how much better? I'm not sure.

ROBBRECHT – The pictures are not bad. But instead of there being no furniture, there are no cars. I think this is quite a modest project. It's not *the* bridge over the motorway, the one you'll remember for the rest of your life.

CONROY – But it's a better bridge. It is clever and elegant. It's thoughtful, but has not been able to colonise the bridge and setting.

BETSKY – The only thing that's elegant is the strut. It's not enough. If you put this in the exhibition, you say this is good architecture.

ROBBRECHT – If you were passing by it you might not see it, but I really would keep it in.

FINUCANE – I think I'd pass by it and not notice it. I just don't see what is in it that is remarkable and exciting and innovative and design-based, all those things we've talked about as the criteria. I just don't see it.

BETSKY – I'm also thinking about the message it gives if you put this in an exhibition.

O'NEILL – But what's happening is that we are building really, really dreadful things. I suppose what we are saying, the thing about drawing attention to something is saying we commend you on your consideration in this project. This is different and better.

ROUGHAN & O'DONOVAN – established in 1974. Major projects include the M1 Motorway / Drogheda Bypass with the cable-stayed Boyne Bridge, and elements of the Luas light rail system in Dublin, including Taney Bridge, Dundrum.
GRAFTON ARCHITECTS – established in 1977. (See p46 for full biography.)
DESIGN TEAM – Joe O'Donovan (project director), Nigel O'Neill (preliminary design), Marc Jones (detailed design), John O'Driscoll (project technician), with Grafton Architects (assistant architect: Miriam Dunn)

ROUGHAN & O'DONOVAN ENGINEERS, Arena House, Arena Road, Sandyford, Dublin 18.
T 01-2940800 / F 01-2940820 / E info@rod.ie / W www.roughanodonovan.com

GRAFTON ARCHITECTS, 12 Dame Court, Dublin 2
T 01-6713365 / F 01-6713178 / E info@graftonarchitects.ie

IN-BETWEEN HOUSE, Ballinamore, Co Leitrim

Dominic Stevens Architect

In-between – The circulation spaces, the leftover spaces, the common spaces in buildings, are areas where the user finds an open programme, a temporary void in time, space and function. These spaces lie in-between defined areas of activity. Children are sent to school to sit in classrooms and learn, yet it is in the corridors that they acquire their most valuable skill – how to negotiate society. Ultimately, in the in-between space, it is up to you to take control and decide what to do. What better place to read than on the stairs?

House – This house is for a couple who work from home, and their two children. They decided to move from central Dublin to a hillside overlooking a lake in Leitrim. The house has two kinds of spaces. The first has distinct functions – sleeping, cooking, working, bathing – each in a separate block. These rooms are a defined shape: they have four walls; you know whether you are within the room or outside it; they envelop you and protect you. Their individual shapes force you to be aware of the walls, the edges of the enclosure. They require conscious evaluation of shape and size. The windows and doors in these walls give framed views of the landscape. Between these flow an in-between living/connecting space. It is in this in-between space that the unprogrammed activity goes on, the general stuff of living. These all flow into one another. How they are used is reinvented day after day. Hillside becomes entrance space becomes reading corner becomes gathering space. These are spaces that, although charged with atmosphere, are not particular in their suggested use – like a forest clearing or a hilltop plateau.

A *Place in the Landscape* – The house is made of pieces that have a scale and material simplicity akin to rural Irish vernacular houses. This collection of pieces sits in the landscape like a traditional settlement of house and outbuildings. The pieces capture a fluid moment in the landscape – a collection of terraces where the in-between space happens.

Area – 200m². Stage – completed 2003.

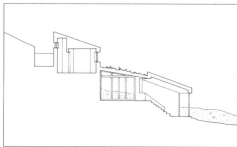

Section AA

Function drawing

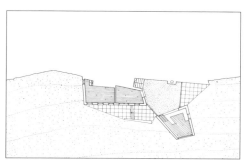

Lower level plan

Site plan

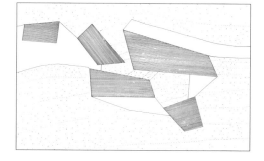

Roof Plan

Upper level plan

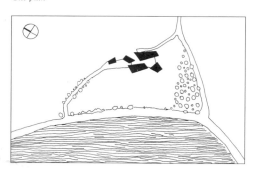

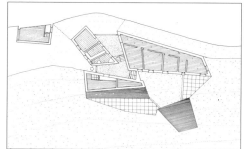

ASSESSORS' COMMENTS

BETSKY – There are two things I liked about this. One is that it reminds me of the Charles Moore scheme for Sea Ranch, which is one of my favourites, specifically for the condominiums. And the second is I like this kind of tumbling living room, staircase, the in-between spaces. Those were quite nice. What concerns me – and I think it will be a lot better when it's more embedded in the landscape – is the detailing and the relationship of this house to the ground. Round the edges it really starts to fray. It has got the eye-catching image right, and it's got this one space that tumbles down and expands, and then everything else seems not so well done. Then you look at the mannerisms of the plan, and you think, does there have to be all those funny angles?

CONROY – The fragmented geometry doesn't bring much beyond a picturesque composition. The rooms all ultimately look the same. There's not much variety in volume, or in the quality of them. The window shapes are pretty consistent throughout. I think the opes aren't that carefully placed. The junction of the two stairs with that little half-wall is unresolved. If you think about, say, what could have happened in the gaps between the blocks in terms of taking light in... that's what Charles Moore would have done. Those volumes would have spiralled up as well as out, and I don't think any of that's been achieved. There's a predictability about the detailing, the volumes and the windows that I think weaken the conceit of its fragmentation.

O'NEILL – The only thing is that because we have this issue about rural housing and housing in the landscape, it's beginning to at least examine that and attempt something specific.

ROBBRECHT – It looks like an Irish house, the image that I have of Irish houses on the west coast. It has this presence that is very acceptable.

FINUCANE – It's also attempting to do something that is vaguely within the vernacular, but contemporary. I'd consider it really, because they are problems and issues here in Ireland that it is trying to address.

CONROY – And it's courageous in addressing that.

BETSKY – Really? When you have the budget to make a single family house on a large site like that, I wonder how much courage you really need.

FINUCANE – Well, this is social courage and political courage.

BETSKY – It's funny. It's like you want to combine some of those houses that are spatially nothing and yet detailed to death, together with this one, which has spatial potential but is short on detail.

DOMINIC STEVENS – born in 1965. Graduated from UCD in 1989. Worked in Berlin with Christoph Langhof and Leipe Steigelman (1990-95). In private practice since 1995. Studio tutor at UCD. Published *Domestic* in 1995, a book about designing the home. Recipient of AAI Awards and Special Mentions for various buildings.
BRIAN WARD – graduated from UCD School of Architecture in 1992. Has worked in Berlin, Dublin, New York and Leitrim. Studio tutor at UCD.

DOMINIC STEVENS ARCHITECT
Cloone, Co Leitrim – T 071-9636988 / F 071-9636134

PHOTOGRAPHIC CREDITS

NEW IRISH ARCHITECTURE / AAI AWARDS SERIES

For nineteen years, the *New Irish Architecture* series has been comprehensively documenting the best of contemporary Irish architecture through the buildings and projects featured in the annual AAI Awards. Each volume carries copious drawings and photographs, architects' descriptions and assessors' comments on every awarded or commended scheme.

"This annual showing of the best architectural projects in Ireland ... seems to get more and more accessible to the non-expert, which is the way it should be. It is now a fascinating book that opens the whole world of creative architecture to the layman." — BOOKS IRELAND

"A lively look at what's newest in Irish architecture which is generating a lot of excitement. The judges' comments and accompanying texts make the photographs and drawings easy to follow." — SUNDAY TRIBUNE

ORDER FORM

The *New Irish Architecture* series can be ordered from any good bookshop or direct from Gandon Editions (same-day dispatch; postage free in Ireland, worldwide at cost). Order by phone, fax, e-mail or post.

Please send me: *(other volumes are out of print)*

____ New Irish Architecture 8 – AAI Awards 1993   €10   ____ New Irish Architecture 16 – AAI Awards 2001   €20

____ New Irish Architecture 12 – AAI Awards 1997   €10   ____ New Irish Architecture 17 – AAI Awards 2002   €20

____ New Irish Architecture 13 – AAI Awards 1998   €10   ____ New Irish Architecture 18 – AAI Awards 2003   €20

____ New Irish Architecture 15 – AAI Awards 2000   €10   ____ New Irish Architecture 19 – AAI Awards 2004   €20

❏ payment enclosed by cheque € / stg £ / US $ _____   ❏ please charge my Laser/Mastercard/Visa   [MasterCard] [VISA]

— — — — — — — — — — — — — — — — — — — —   expiry __ __ / __ __   security code __ __ __

name _____   PRINT NAME & ADDRESS

address _____

_____   TRADE: order # _____   contact _____   S/R

The New Irish Architecture *series is produced and distributed for the AAI by Gandon Editions, the largest producer and distributor of books on Irish art and architecture. Our colour catalogue carries full details of these and other architecture titles.*

GANDON EDITIONS   Oysterhaven, Kinsale, Co Cork, Ireland
T +353 (0)21-4770830 / F 021-4770755 / E gandon@eircom.net   4/04